The Lore of the Camino de Santiago

A Literary Pilgrimage

Best Regards + Many Thanks !

Jean Mitchell-Lanham

The Lore of the Camino de Santiago

A Literary Pilgrimage

Jean Mitchell-Lanham

Two Harbors Press
Minneapolis, MN

Every myth or legend begins with a seed of truth.

Acknowledgments

No one deserves more recognition than my husband, who stayed at home with our two Dalmatians, Finnegan and Buttons, while I trekked across Spain for six weeks gathering information on the Camino de Santiago. He also graciously read my drafts and gave some very insightful suggestions.

Thanks go to my brother-in-law, Bob Lanham. While I walked in the footsteps of all those pilgrims who had gone before me, Bob handled all my email transmittals to my computer-illiterate, technophobic husband.

I would also like to remember my graduate professor and thesis advisor, Aristóbulo Pardo, who shared his love and knowledge of the Spanish medieval literature with me at The Ohio State University during my graduate studies there. He has since passed from this world, but I image him sitting in a library somewhere still poring over manuscripts from past ages.

Thanks too, to all those wonderful pilgrims, the ones I met through stories and the ones I met physically, who made the trek a little easier.

Finally, special thanks to that "son of thunder," warrior, missionary, apostle and pilgrim, who truly made this book possible: Saint James.

Contents

Introduction

Travelers, there is no path, paths are made by walking.
—Antonio Machado

There are many books written about the *Camino de Santiago*, known as *The Way of Saint James* or *Road to Santiago* in English. Sometimes this route is referred to as the *Camino Francés* (*French Route*). The route is famous due to several things but mainly because the route leads to Santiago de Compostela where Saint James, the apostle, is honored in a beautiful gothic cathedral. Moreover, many Christians believe that Saint James not only brought the Christian faith to Spain but that his martyred body was found in Spain in the early 800s and now lies in the cathedral where people can view his tomb. Devout Christians believe that they can be redeemed of their sins or cured of afflictions through the help of Saint James. During the Middle Ages word spread of James's miracles and drew pilgrims to his shrine for many centuries.

Pilgrims have walked this route for over a thousand years to visit the tomb of Saint James or Santiago as he is known in Spanish. (Saint James is also known as Saint James, the Greater.) Pilgrims during medieval times were able to gain forgiveness for all their sins by making the pilgrimage. Some pilgrims were former criminals and were forced to make the pilgrimage as part of their sentences. Today's pilgrim does the pilgrimage for a variety of reasons and religion still plays a part for a large majority. Others go for the hiking experience, exercise or just to commune with nature. For whatever reason they choose, the experience will be one that leaves an indelible memory in their lives.

While there is no single route to Santiago, the Camino Francés is the oldest, most popular route and it eventually merges with other routes from Spain, Portugal, France and other countries of Europe. The French route runs from Saint-Jean-Pied-de-Port on the French side of the Pyrenees to Roncesvalles on the Spanish side and then extends another four hundred and sixty-eight miles (780 km) passing through the major cities of Pamplona, Logroño, Burgos, León and Astorga before reaching the city of Santiago de Compostela. A typical walk on the Camino Francés takes at least four to five weeks, allowing for one or two rest days on the way. The actual end of the Camino is at *Finisterre* (*End of the World*), where many pilgrims continue on after visiting Santiago. You will learn why they do this later on in the book.

While the word *camino* means *road*, the word should not be taken literally because in many places the Camino is nothing more than a narrow footpath. Moreover, the word camino is used constantly when meeting other pilgrims. Pilgrims on the Camino traditionally greet each other with the words, *buen camino*, which convey the meaning similar to *have a good trip* or *have a good journey*, similar to the French phrase, *bon voyage*. When pilgrims need to ask directions or the distance and time from one stage to the next, the word camino is used. When pilgrims spot the yellow markers pointing in the direction toward Santiago, they know they are on the Camino even if they are standing on a two-foot-wide path. By the end of the journey the word camino becomes semi-sacred and metaphorical for most pilgrims, and they find the word has a whole new and distinct meaning for them.

Sometimes you may hear the old Latin greeting given by pilgrims in the Middle Ages. A single word was used as a greeting then, and it was *ultreia* or *ultreya*. It was a word of encouragement to the weary pilgrim and meant, *keep on going* or *go for it*. The greeting is not as popular today as the *buen camino* greeting, but you may still hear it occasionally.

Pilgrims along with non-pilgrims have been traveling the Camino for centuries. Imaginary characters too, such as Chaucer's "Wife of Bath," are described as having made a pilgrimage to Santiago. Real people, such as Margery Kempe, an English woman (1373–1438) credited with writing the first autobiography in English, made several pilgrimages in her lifetime. One such pilgrimage was to Santiago de Compostela. Kings, popes, and saints also made the pilgrimage. King Louis VII of France made the journey in 1154. Popes John Paul II, John XXIII and Benedict XVI have visited the shrine. Pope Benedict XVI actually walked the last twenty-two miles of the Camino to Santiago. Saints such as Francis of Assisi and Brigid of Sweden journeyed to Santiago to honor Saint James.

The zenith for pilgrimages to Santiago occurred between 900-1350. The reasons for this are multiple. Of course, the initial catalyst was the discovery of Saint James's tomb around 814 by a hermit, and the subsequent authentication by the local bishop. The construction of a church and later the cathedral attracted Christians from all over Europe. Besides, it was no longer safe to travel to the premier pilgrimage spot, Jerusalem, because it fell under control of the Muslims during part of the eleventh and twelfth centuries. This was also a period when the cult of relics played an important role in the life of medieval man. Relics were divided into first and second classes. A body part was much more important than a piece of clothing from the saint. Such relics would be put on display at the shrine or encased in a tomb where devotees could touch or kiss the container. The majority of shrines did not have an entire body of a saint, as Santiago de Compostela proclaimed to have. An entire body would be a greater enticement to make a pilgrimage to a shrine that had one. Furthermore, this over 1,000-year-old pilgrimage was considered, and is still considered today, as one of the three pilgrimages on which all sins can be forgiven, Rome and Jerusalem being the other two.

Another reason for the rise in popularity of this pilgrimage was the legendary Battle of Clavijo, said to have taken place in the early 800s. Saint James comes down from the sky on a magnificent white steed and defeats the Moorish army. From this battle Saint James receives the moniker, *Santiago Matamoros* (*Saint James the Moor Slayer*). While this event is based on legend, the supposed battle has provided one of the strongest ideological icons in the Spanish national identity. More about the Battle of Clavijo comes in a later chapter.

Still another reason for the rise in popularity for this particular pilgrimage during the Middle Ages was the institution of the Knights of Santiago. Instituted in the late twelfth century, these knights offered protection to the pilgrims. They provided lodging, food, and hospitals as well as tended to their religious needs. One of the most grandiose hospitals still stands today in the city of Santiago. Of course, it is no longer a hospital but has been converted to one of Spain's signature landmarks, a *parador* (a historical building such as a castle or manor house, that has been converted and restored to use as a luxury hotel). The busy Queen Isabella, who sponsored Columbus's voyages to America, kicked the Jews and Moors out of Spain and instituted the malevolent Inquisition all in the year 1492, somehow still made time to build this hospital in the same year. Today it is called the *Hotel Reyes Católicos* (*Catholic Monarchs Hotel*). Few pilgrims stay at the hotel because of the price, but tradition still holds that a pilgrim can get a free meal in the onsite pilgrim's dining facility at a designated time.

Another group of knights, the Templars, were also protectors of the pilgrims. However, because of severe persecution in France, due mainly to political and monetary reasons, they were accused of heresy and the last Grand Master, James of Molay, was burned at the stake in 1314. They soon disbanded and until very recently were considered to be guilty of heresy and therefore not acknowledged by the Church. Recent discoveries in the Vatican Archives have proved the hersey accusations to be untrue. A document known as the *Chinon Parchment*, found in 2001, records Pope Clement V's verdict that the Templars were not guilty of heresy. In spite of their demise they managed to resurrect themselves under different names. In Portugal they were known as the *Ordem dos Cavaleiros de Nosso Senhor Jesus Cristo* (*Order of Christ*). In regards to the Camino, you can still visit one of their magnificent castles that lies on the Camino in the town of Ponferrada. Within the castle walls is a library that contains a wonderful collection of illuminated manuscripts and is well worth a visit.

The construction of bridges and road maintenance also played an important role in making the Camino more inviting to the pilgrims. Road maintenance became the undertaking of *Santo Domingo de la Calzada* (*Saint Dominic of the Road*). In addition to his road improvements and maintenance, he built lodgings and bridges.

The last reason and not the least one for the increase in popularity of this pilgrimage was the medieval illuminated manuscript, known by two names: *Liber de Sancti Jacobi* or *Codex Calixtinus*. I will discuss this manuscript in greater detail throughout our journey; suffice it to say at this time, scholars believe the authors are multiple since the manuscript consists of five separate books and multiple writing styles. Book V is touted as the first guidebook in Europe. Do not be misled by that proclamation because no pilgrim would want to carry a tome that must weigh about ten pounds. Nor would the everyday pilgrim have access to such a document. A pilgrim would have to visit one of the monasteries that had a copy and he or she would not only have to know how to read but know how to read Latin.

The decline of the pilgrimage to Santiago started in the mid fourteenth century and lasted till the late twentieth century. The first decline came with the Black Death. Then came the Protestant Reformation that frowned on things such as plenary indulgences and relics, things associated with the pilgrimage. Continuous warfare would also keep people at home. Spain seemed to have more than its fair share of wars with France and England from the 1500s onward. The early nineteenth century saw less than fifty pilgrims a year. Spain would also engage in war with the U.S. in 1898 in Cuba and the Philippines. Two world wars and Spain's civil war in 1936–39 would tend to discourage pilgrims. Neither would Franco's dictatorship nor the Basque terrorist movement of the mid twentieth century induce people to travel the Camino. A major portion of the French route passes through the Basque province, which had an intimidating effect on traveling through this area. Thus, a onetime European attraction, the pilgrimage fell into decline for centuries.

It has been only fairly recently (1990s) that the pilgrimage to Santiago regained the popularity it had in the Middle Ages. This is due in part to a Spanish priest, Father D. Elias Valiña Sampedro, who wrote his dissertation in the mid-1960s on the origin and history of the Camino. He is responsible for the yellow arrows and shell markers that show the way to Santiago. Working with local communities along the Camino, he was able to organize lodging facilities and pilgrim centers that help pilgrims overcome difficulties. Difficulties such as needing medical attention for those sore feet and other ailments, or just giving information to pilgrims on where to find lodging, food or an ATM are just a few ways these centers assist today's pilgrims.

Other factors that have influenced the growth of the pilgrimage are the rediscovery of *Liber Sancti Jacobi/Codex Calixtinus*, containing an early Camino guidebook, and the plethora of modern guidebooks that have been published that focus on a variety of interests that should appeal to the most reluctant pilgrim. Being declared a World Heritage Site by UNESCO in 1987 is also a draw factor. There are over 1,800 historical sites on the Camino to command the attention of history buffs, ordinary tourists, and the devout pilgrims.

Many books written by pilgrims and even a movie (*The Way*) have helped popularize the pilgrimage, especially for North Americans. According to the website, peregrinossantiago.es, 192,488 pilgrims registered with the *Oficina de Peregrino* (*Pilgrim's Office*) in Santiago in 2012. Of those, 7,071 were from the United States of America or approximately 3.67 percent of the total. In 2013, the numbers rose to 215,880 pilgrims and the US number rose to 10,125 or 4.69 percent of the total number to walk the Camino, up 1.02 percent over the previous year. The USA is increasing in numbers but still lags behind many other European groups of pilgrims.

Another enlightening film, a documentary called *Walking The Camino: Six Ways to Santiago,* has won numerous film awards including "Outstanding Achievement in Documentary Filmmaking" at the Newport Beach Film Festival and "Best Documentary" at the Hollywood Film Festival. It is a well-done film and should be seen by anyone contemplating the Camino. I saw it after walking the Camino and wished I had seen it before the trip (it wasn't released until after my trip).

Many books describe in detail the topography of this ancient route, from departure points such as Saint-Jean-Pied-de-Port in France to the tomb of Saint James in Santiago and beyond to the end of the Camino in Finisterre. Some of these books cover weather, lodging, shrines, costs, time, distances, food and points of interests. Because these items are subject to change, one would do well to check the internet for the latest information. In addition, a little common sense will work wonders for having a more pleasant experience. For example, my Travel Tip #1: travel light. Take more money and fewer clothes. Travel Tip #2: be prepared for rainy weather in northern Spain. Moreover, it is not my intention to write another traditional guidebook for the Camino. Instead, I hope to take the reader through areas of the Camino to get an inside glance of where legends and literature were born.

I spent a lot of time researching the route via books, the internet and people who had done the trek. I also did the trek from Saint-Jean-Pied-de-Port to Santiago in 2013. What I learned was overwhelming. The medieval atmosphere is still there among the small towns and villages; prices fluctuate from what is reported in guidebooks; some *albergues* (*pilgrim lodgings*) are no longer open and new ones are present for evaluation; weather is unpredictable; time has a whole new meaning in Spain (read up on business hours and mealtimes so you won't be disappointed when you find the stores close at 1 or 2 in the afternoon and do not reopen until 5 or 6 pm, or are closed on Mondays, or the restaurants don't open until 2); and if you are a vegan, you might have a problem since seafood (in Galicia) and meat (in Basque country) are the biggies here, along with wine. The route passes through Rioja, one of the most famous wine-producing areas in Spain. Knowing that autumn is the time of grape harvesting and wine festivals may help you decide what time of year you do this trek. And no, that is not why I chose to go in September.

I chose to go in September because the weather is *generally* better. I emphasize the word *generally* because the weather in the Pyrenees has been known to change dramatically within minutes. The other reason I chose September is because it is less crowded. No noisy school kids to deal with. Most people have done their vacations by this time, too. This makes lodging and restaurants much more accessible. (I never had a problem finding either of these. I highly recommend the website: mundicamino.com. You can select the route and language you prefer and do searches for numerous items such as lodging, restaurants, drugstores, etc. I found most of my lodgings through this site. With this recommendation, however, there is a caveat. The English translations for some of the items are terribly unprofessional. They may cause you to start pulling your hair out or break into hysterical laughter. Either way you still will probably get the gist of what is intended. Remember too, websites may have some outdated information. When I found an item such as a lodging on mundicamino.com that I wanted to book or check out, I went directly to that lodging's website for verification and a more in depth search of the item.)

People go on this pilgrimage for a variety of reasons: religious, midlife crisis, a need for adventure, etc. If given a multiple-choice test on why I made this pilgrimage, I would probably choose "all of the above." However, my main reason goes back to my college days when I was living and studying in Madrid. During that year, I fell in love with the culture, people and country, even though I was there during the Franco dictatorship when censorship was at its height and there was a lot of repression. I learned from that experience to appreciate the true meaning of freedom. I remember reading newspapers and books that had entire paragraphs blacked out. Movies had scenes muted if they were considered politically incorrect. Also during this time, travelers were warned of potential dangers in the Basque region due to terrorist activities, so I did not get an opportunity to visit those areas that would have enriched my studies of the Spanish Middle Ages and its literature. These places still exist on the Camino and I now had an opportunity to see these places that have enriched the Camino with legends, folklore and literary genre. What better way to encounter them than to follow the old pilgrim route and find their connection to it.

Since I studied Spanish language and literature, and in particular, the medieval period, I decided to research the Camino area for its literature in general, not just the medieval period. I started researching the idea of connecting the Camino with literature and folklore produced in this area of five hundred-plus miles, a journey I was not able to do during my student years. The route was not as popular then as it was during medieval times, and as it is today. More importantly, the route was not clearly marked like it is currently. (Even with the yellow arrows and scallop shell signs, I managed to get lost twice. I wouldn't want to attempt this trek without them.) Of course, the Basque unrest that I mentioned earlier was clearly a deterrent. However, looking back on this aspect, it is quite ironic because most of the Basque terrorism took place in Madrid where I was living and it was targeted mostly toward government officials.

In looking back I really should not have been so concerned about the unrest. After all, medieval pilgrims faced far more dangers, such as marauding Moors, robbers, wild wolf packs, unscrupulous innkeepers and cheating toll-takers, to name a few. They didn't have the path markers and there was only one guidebook which was only available in monasteries, and not readily accessible to the common pilgrim.

To return to my earlier statement: What I aim to do in this book is craft a literary pilgrimage and share with you the works and their authors (if known) associated directly or indirectly with the pilgrimage route. Hopefully, these works will make the pilgrimage much more meaningful to the walking pilgrim as well as the armchair pilgrim. A pilgrim will be able to recall the stories and relate to a specific place as he or she passes through them. On the other hand, the armchair pilgrims might find these literary ventures so intriguing that they will want to walk the Camino in order to see and enjoy the discovery of these places for themselves. In addition, my aim is to entertain as well as inform the pilgrim-reader/walker in much the same way as the medieval pilgrims entertained each other with stories while they travelled along the Camino. Somewhat like Chaucer's tales, there are tales of knights, and a nun. And unlike Chaucer there are tales of an evil innkeeper, an evil innkeeper's daughter, resuscitated roasted chickens, and a slew of miraculous tales performed by Saint James and the Virgin Mary that will stir your range of emotions from tears to hysterical laughter. The existence of more modern literature also exists on the Camino and it too will make its appearance as we travel this road.

As a means of clarification, works directly associated with the route are those that involve the Camino. They can be written, visual, or orally transcribed works, including legends, myths, folktales, novels and poetry. Those indirectly associated with the Camino are those works that were composed somewhere on or near the route but not always associated with the pilgrimage. All of the stories have somehow left their influence on the Camino. From time to time, I may leave the main path to seek one of the shrines or monasteries that pilgrims also seek out because of the legends, miracles, and/or oral folklore connected to them. One of the monasteries in particular had a great effect on the Spanish language, but that comes later. These places are never more than a few kilometers from the main route and well worth the side trip.

I should add that I started this adventure by flying to Paris from San Francisco, California, on September 4, 2013. I arrived in Paris, September 5th, and took the train to Bayonne. I stayed overnight and the next morning (now Sept. 6), I caught the train for Saint-Jean-Pied-de-Port where I spent the night. Having made prior arrangements to meet with an Alaskan acquaintance in Saint Jean, I started the five hundred-plus-mile trek at about 7 am on September 7th. I completed the trek to Santiago on Oct. 5th.

Now, my dear reader, let the adventure begin!

Jean Mitchell-Lanham
Pacifica, California
November 2013

Chapter 1

Shouts of *"Monjoie!"*

Originally I had intended to do the trek alone, but because my husband was worried about my well-being I relented and agreed to meet his friend's wife who was an experienced hiker and wanted to do this trek. I was introduced to Julie when she and her husband Steve were on a trip to California. They visited us in our home and we discussed our ideas concerning the trip. I had no problem in accepting Julie as a traveling companion. She is a gracious and delightful person. Julie returned to her home in Alaska and we kept in contact via email making our plans for the upcoming trip. We knew going into this that on the Camino it is quite common for people to start out together yet not finish together. Sometimes it is due to illness, incompatibility, or different objectives. Julie had a shorter timeframe than I did and wanted to finish as quickly as possible. We both wanted to do side trips that were not compatible. Therefore, we went our separate ways once we reached Burgos, which was about twelve days into the trek. Julie completed the trek a couple of days ahead of me. We did get together again in Madrid after completing the trek and had a delightful meal where we talked about our experiences on the Camino.

Now that I have explained the appearance and disappearance of my traveling companion, I'll get to the adventure. We started our journey on September 7th by checking out of the Hotel Itzalpea, which lies just outside the walled portion of the town of Saint-Jean-Pied-de-Port. We passed through the main entrance, the *Porte Saint Jacques* (*Saint James Gate*), full of confidence and thrilled to be off on this adventure. Because my friend walks at a much faster pace, we agreed to walk at our own pace and meet at our next lodging that evening. I didn't mind walking alone, and others who had done the trek told me never to change my pace to accommodate someone else. It has become my Pilgrim Tip #3: Always go at your own pace.

Even though Julie walked at a faster pace, I usually reached the lodging first because she stopped in the afternoon to have a picnic lunch and a nap, which involved an hour or more break. I always kept walking, except for a fifteen- or twenty-minute lunch break at a café or bar on route, where I could use the facilities and get water.

My first goal was to get to Roncesvalles in time to check out the town's historical spots. This meant at least an eight-hour climb over the Pyrenees. It didn't bother me that I was facing an uphill climb to over 4,000 feet. It was the downhill of the last three miles that I feared would be the most treacherous, and be my demise. Actually, it was not so bad. I took it very slowly, sometimes walking sideways to protect my toes from having a jam session due to the force of downward acceleration.

What was worse was the weather change I encountered a third of the way up the mountain. Talk about weather changes—who could have predicted the following would happen all within a couple of hours? First it started to rain rather intensely. I quickly pulled out my poncho and enshrouded myself with it. Next began the thunder and lightning show. I was told during such a storm that there were these little huts you could crawl into for safety. Of course, I never found them until after the storm. When the thunderstorm abated then came hail and flash floods. I thought I might panic, but having to concentrate on walking helped me avoid it. I don't know where all the water came from but it was gushing from everywhere. It was like somebody pulled the plug out of the dike. I managed to climb to higher ground as the path below washed out. Finally I found a part of the main path again, but now a new menace arrived. FOG! Normally, I have no fear of fog (I live in the Fog Belt near San Francisco), but this one came on so quickly and so thickly that it erased any trace of landscape around me; moreover, this was unfamiliar landscape to me. A whiteout as far as I could see! I kept repeating my mantra learned from my days as a safety diver in underwater exploration. "Don't panic, panic kills!"

As I walked I kept my eyes cast down trying to see the ground and make sure I was still on the path. I used my walking poles to feel for solid ground since the path was very narrow in some areas and I did not want to go tumbling down the mountainside. I did not see or hear anyone else on the path. I was so intent on looking at the ground that I almost ended up smacking the rear end of a huge horse that was standing in the center of the path. I gasped out of fright and managed to miss its rear end. Recovering from this near mishap, I started to chuckle thinking of all the ass-kissing I'd seen over the years, especially in places where I had worked. In retrospect, this was the closest I'd ever come to kissing a real horse's ass.

The horse was gargantuan, something like a miniature Clydesdale (or maybe a Belgian), with "thunder thighs" that would have sent me tumbling down the mountainside with one slight bump. The horse wasn't wearing any gear, not even the usual neck bell that the herders put on their livestock so they can find them in the storms and fog. I concluded it must be one of the wild horses that roam these mountains. Cautiously I moved by this behemoth. Talking softly as I went, I wanted to reach out and touch this magnificent creature but refrained from doing so. Instead I turned around, backing away so we were face to face. I continued backing my way down the path, feeling the ground with my poles, and as I did, I stopped to blow a kiss to this magnificent animal. With a silent sigh of relief I continued my trek.

During this brief encounter I was so preoccupied with the horse that I failed to notice the fog lifting and a ray of sun began to show. What a relief! Pilgrim Travel Tip #3: On a trek, never leave home without your walking poles. They are great navigating tools in a heavy fog, great for stopping downhill acceleration, handy for keeping your balance, and a decent defensive weapon if needed.

Looking ahead on the trail I saw the forest give way to open space and lots of spectacular views. I reached a spot where there were several pilgrims seated on the ground having lunch. And of all things there was a lunch wagon parked near this grassy spot. I noticed a side road that joined the path I was on, so I deduced that was how the lunch wagon had arrived there. I meandered over to the lunch wagon, bought a few items and then inquired what a lunch wagon was doing there. The nice man in the wagon told me he always came there because it was the pilgrimage's highest point before descending to Roncesvalles; apparently, most pilgrims took a rest and some refreshment by the time they reached this spot. Then it dawned on me that I had reached Col de Lepoeder Pass or 4,350 feet, the highest point in elevation on this leg of the trek. I was almost to Roncesvalles, only about three miles to go. I wanted to shout *"monjoie,"*[1] the medieval French rallying cry of soldiers in the heat of battle. I had conquered a mountain. Monjoie!

During my rest at Col de Lepoeder, I began to reflect back on the history of this road to Santiago. I wondered about the number of pilgrims who had crossed the Pyrenees and perhaps had sat right here gazing at the valleys below, as I did that afternoon. Then I thought of the Romans who came this way and built parts of the road and bridges that I would walk on shortly. Napoleon's invading armies crossed here too, on their way to rule Spain. During World War II, downed

---

1   The etymology of the term varies with interpreters. It is first recorded in the Song of Roland (twelfth century). One interpreter suggests that it is a term for marking stones or cairns set up on the roadside. From about 1200 it appears in French as *monjoie*. Also connected is the name, *Mons Gaudii*, given by medieval pilgrims to Rama, a point northwest of Jerusalem, from the top of which approaching pilgrims would get their first glance of the city. The meaning related to, *my joy*, seems most appropriate when linked to reaching a goal such as the end of a pilgrimage, victory in battle, or conquering a mountain.

British and American pilots used this route to escape from the Germans with the aid of Basque resistant fighters.

Because of my literary background, the most poignant image I had as I sat on this mountaintop was the return of Charlemagne's army to France and the loss of his favorite knight, Roland, at the Battle of Roncesvalles. The famous French epic poem, "Chanson de Roland," written in the mid twelfth century, immortalizes these events that occurred in the eighth century, that is, the return to France, the Battle at Roncesvalles and much more. It gives the aware pilgrim a sense of seeing, hearing and feeling a bygone time. I could almost hear Roland and his soldiers shouting the great battle cry, "monjoie," as they are said to have done on that fateful day in 778 in the same valley below me. Then I related to the lines in the poem where Charlemagne waited for Roland and experienced similar weather to what I had earlier in the morning. The lines 1424–1427, strophe 110, recall our mutual experience:

Orez i ad de tuneire e de vent,
Pluies e gresilz desmesureement;
Chiedent i fuildres e menut e suvent,
E terremoete ço i ad veirement.[2]

Thunder and windstorms,
Rain and hail to excess;
Lightning strikes in rapid succession over and over again,
Indeed there is an earthquake.

---

2   Gerard J. Brault's, *La Chanson de Roland, Oxford Text and English Translation* (Pennsylvania State University, 1997) pp. 88–9. All quotes (French and English) are taken from this edition.

The only thing I didn't experience, that Charlemagne did, was an earthquake, but the thought crossed my mind when the hail started pelting me and the lightning streaked repeatedly across the sky. I didn't know if there were any active volcanoes in the area, but I am sure if there were, one would have erupted. As it turned out, this was the worst weather I encountered during the whole trip. Had I encountered much more of this type of weather, I do not think that I would have completed the trek.

The battle that was taking place between Roland and the Moors while Charlemagne waited out the weather near Roncesvalles was lost by Roland due to his insatiable pride. He not only lost the battle but his life too. He was too proud to sound his horn to signal that he needed help. The old proverb, "Pride goeth before the fall," was never so apropos as it was on that sad day for Charlemagne's favorite knight.

Some other lines from the poem covering the battle came to mind as I sat there on the mountaintop. In remembering them, the landscape of the peaceful valley below transformed into the horrific battleground of Roland's encounter with the Moors. Freeing my imagination, it didn't take much to picture the battle scene described in strophe 93, beginning with line 1197. The shouts and screams of fallen warriors and their horses echoed in my head. Roland slayed the Moor, Aelroth, in a furious and gory struggle: *(Warning: the following poetic lines contain rather graphic images and may not be suitable for all ages. They may even disturb you—not likely, since our modern-day video games, movies, and TV programs are just as bad, if not worse, and are also required to post such a caveat. I feel obliged to do so too, even though it is done with tongue in cheek. Caveat lector!)*

Sun cheval brochet, laiset curre a esforz,
Vait le ferir li quens quanque il pout.
L'escut li freint e l'osberc li desclot,
Trenchet le piz, si li briset les os,
Tute l'eschine li desevret del dos,
Od sun espiet l'anme li getet fors,
Enpeint le ben, fait li brandir le cors,
Pleine sa hanste del cheval l'abat mort,
En dous meitiez li ad briset le col.

He (Roland) spurs his horse; he lets him run full speed,
The Count (Aelroth) goes to strike him with all his might.
He smashes his shield and tears open his hauberk,
Cuts into his breast and shatters his bones,
He severs his spine from the back,
He thrusts out his soul with his spear,
He sticks it deeply into him; he impales his whole body,
Running him through, he throws him dead from his horse,
He has broken his neck in two halves.

Again in strophe 104, lines 1325–1334:

Sun cheval brochet, si vait ferir Chernuble.
L'elme li freint u li carbuncle luisent,
Trenchet le cors e la cheveleüre,
Si li trenchat les oilz e la faiture,
Le blanc osberc, dunt la maile est menue,
E tut le cors tresqu'en la furcheüre,
Enz en la sele, ki est a or batue,
El cheval est l'espee aresteüe;
Trenchet l'eschine, hunc n'i out quis jointure,
Tut abat mort el pred sur l'erbe drue.

He spurs his horse and goes to strike Chernuble.
He smashes his helmet where the carbuncles glow,
He hacks through the body and the scalp,

He hacked through his eyes and his face,
Through the shiny hauberk, whose chain mail is close-meshed.
Through his entire body down to the crotch,
Through the saddle, which is wrought with gold.
The sword has come to rest in the horse;
He hacks through the spine, he never sought out a joint,
He throws him dead in the meadow on the thick grass.

Soon after the Battle of Roncesvalles in 778, troubadours began composing songs about the battle and the events surrounding it. These became known as *chansons de geste* (*songs of heroic deeds*) and were handed down from one generation to another orally and eventually written down at a much later date. Of course, they changed with each composer adding his own embellishments or interpretation. It may be, too, that the composer had a faulty memory or a hearing problem, which would create end results similar to kids playing the game of "telephone" (that is, a group of kids form a line and the first kid whispers a word or phrase to the next kid who in turn passes it on until it reaches the last kid). The last kid says the word or phrase aloud and usually it is much changed from the original communiqué. Thus it is easy to understand how events took on different hues as they passed from one generation to another or even from one person to another. In this respect we can understand why there may be many historical inaccuracies and/or inflated accounts of events. However, changing details could have provided encouragement for the political and/or religious agendas of that time period. For example, the unknown poet who wrote the "Chanson de Roland" did not portray history accurately. Roland did not fight Moors at Roncesvalles but

Basque Christians who wanted retribution for Charlemagne's destruction of their city, Pamplona. However, changing the players was advantageous as a political and religious device to encourage bravery, especially among the crusaders and the Christian soldiers fighting for the *Reconquista* (*Reconquest*) of Spain. Knights and soldiers became inflamed with the ideals of Roland's courage and bravery. Another example is William the Conqueror's army. Chroniclers tell of how the "Chanson de Roland" was sung to William's soldiers before the Battle of Hastings to incite them to fight more bravely.[3] (It must have worked because they won the battle.)

By the time of the crusades the Camino was well traveled by pilgrims from different parts of Europe. Part of their entertainment while traveling had been telling stories or singing songs. As they neared Roncesvalles, they most likely would tell or sing of the events that took place there. While the modern-day pilgrim doesn't sing of Roland's deeds, he or she who passes through Roncesvalles will come to know about the famous battle just by visiting the museum containing historical memorabilia about Charlemagne and Roland. One such article you can see is referred to as the *ajedrez de Carlomagno* (*Charlemagne's chessboard*). It looks like a chessboard but it is actually a reliquary where each square on the chessboard contains a relic of some saint or a venerated item. A visit to the *Capilla de Sancti Spiritus* (*Chapel of the Holy Spirit*) will reveal what is reported to be the ossuary or remains of Charlemagne's soldiers killed

---

3   Gerard J. Brault's, *La Chanson de Roland* (Pennsylvania State University, 1997), p. xxv.

in the battle. Along with the soldiers' bones, it is suspected there could be bones of pilgrims too, who may have died near or in Roncesvalles. In addition to these artifacts, the modern-day pilgrim will see the monument to the battle when walking through the town. Despite the historical inaccuracies and embellishments in the poem, its impact on the Camino continues to be present today.

But wait, there's more. Get your fill of Roland and Charlemagne in yet another form of writing that promoted or influenced the popularity of the Camino. These were the manuscripts and chronicles written during the medieval period. One of these was the *Codex Calixtinus,* also known as *Liber de Sancti Jacobi* (*Book of Saint James*). This compilation consists of five separate books, which most scholars now agree were compiled by a French monk, Aymeric Picaud. The *Codex Calixtinus* is housed in the cathedral library of Santiago. It is called the *Codex Calixtinus* (referred to in this book from here on as the *Codex*) mainly because it was said that Pope Calixtinus wrote a letter authorizing it, which is somewhat unnerving since the book was composed after Calixtinus was long gone to his grave. It is widely accepted that it was written and authorized by someone other than this pope.

Another dispute over the authentication of events in Book IV of the *Codex* came into question during the mid-1500s. Ambrosio Morales, a historian, priest and chronicler of some repute for King Philip II, was ordered to visit the various shrines in Spain. His mandate was to check books and relics found in these places. This journey took the better part of 1573–1574. It is said that he was thoroughly disgusted when viewing Book IV of the *Codex* at Santiago de Compostela and said that it would have been better had the book never been written. His opinions and comments in his final report to Philip started heated debates among the intelligentsia. While Ambrosio did not live to see its removal (he died in 1591), Book IV was judged inauthentic and expunged from the *Codex* on the command of King Philip III in 1619.[4] In spite of its removal from the *Codex*, several copies were readily available in various monasteries and continued to be quite popular. The book was finally restored in 1966 to the *Codex* in its original numerical position, that is, Book IV. Because of the removal and restoration of this book, there was sometimes confusion between Books IV and V. Book V became Book IV when the original Book IV was removed and remained so for a long period of time. To clear any confusion, Book IV deals with the stories of Roland and Charlemagne and Book V comprises the first pilgrim's guide to Santiago. Book IV was also known as the *Psuedo Turpin* because the twelfth-century unknown writer tried to pass off his chronicle as the memoirs of Archbishop Turpin of Rheims who just happened to be a contemporary of Charlemagne, which at the time would have lent it some credibility.[5]

Book IV (like the epic poem, the "Chanson de Roland") inflates and embellishes events. Among these events are those that relegate to Charlemagne events that could not

---

4   Manual C. Diaz y Diaz et al., *El Codice Calixtino de la Catedral de Santiago: Estudio codicológico y de contenido* (Santiago de Compostela: Centro de Estudios Jacobeos, 1988), pp. 224–226, 321–325.

5   H.W. Smyser, *The Pseudo Turpin* (Cambridge: The Medieval Academy of America, 1937), p. 1.

possibly be true from a historical viewpoint. In Book IV, Charlemagne is credited with finding the tomb of Saint James. He is visited by Saint James in a vision and told where to find it. He is also credited with being the first pilgrim. The purported tomb of Santiago was found in the early ninth century and a church was constructed around 838 or 839, which Book IV also credits Charlemagne with building. There is only one glitch to this: Charlemagne died in 814. We can understand now why Ambrosio Morales wanted this book removed, especially with credit going to the French for finding Saint James's tomb and building the church. In spite of these inaccuracies in the book, the stories continued to flourish adding fodder to the fire for encouraging the French populace as well as others to undertake the pilgrimage.

Several copies of the *Codex* were made and subsequently found at various monasteries throughout Europe and Asia, including Rome, Jerusalem, Cluny Abbey, and Barcelona. The earliest known edition is in the archives at Santiago de Compostela, which dates from about 1150. The *Codex's* five books are dedicated to the miracles of Saint James, homilies to be used on his feast day, liturgical music compositions and legendary accounts on the origins of the cult of Saint James, the history of Charlemagne and Roland, and the fifth book has been touted as the first tourist guidebook. This fifth book contained valuable information for potential pilgrims, such as where to find lodging, potable water, etc. However, it is not in any sense of the word a guidebook that you could carry around with you, but a rather beautiful, medieval illuminated manuscript. If you were living in the Middle Ages and wanted to read this book, you would have to visit one of the monasteries to gather any necessary information for your pilgrimage. Today you can do the same thing, or purchase a facsimile copy for a hefty price.

Book II and IV of the *Codex* connect us to the Camino in a literary sense. Book II relates the legendary stories of twenty-two miracles that are attributed to Saint James and Book IV shares the epic deeds of Charlemagne and Roland. All twenty-two miracles mention or are directly connected to the pilgrimage to Santiago. Many use the same word "threshold" as synecdoche* for Saint James's basilica and the pilgrimage. The following examples are from the English translation, *The Miracles of Saint James*[6]:

After some time one of them, seeking the threshold of Saint James,… (Miracle 1)

There was no delay: he went to the saint's threshold. (Miracle 3)

Some promised to make a pilgrimage to Saint James's threshold,… (Miracle 9)

Then he set out toward the threshold of Blessed James of Galicia. (Miracle 12)

I met this man myself between Estella and Logroño as he was walking back toward the threshold of Blessed James…(Miracle 22)

We shall see later that many of these same miracles were set to music and/or became poetic compositions in languages

---

* Synecdoche is a figure of speech to which a part is used to represent the whole and the whole for a part.

6   Thomas F. Coffey, Linda Kay Davidson and MaryJane Dunn, *The Miracles of Saint James* (New York: Italica Press, 1996), pp. 61, 63, 75, 78, 96.

other than Latin. But that is for further down the Camino.

Book IV of the *Codex*, as was mentioned previously, is historically inaccurate, and the tales are probably not as intriguing and entertaining to today's world as they were in the Middle Ages. Yet they still lend themselves to today's pilgrims on the Camino. This book relates the arrival of Charlemagne in Spain as well as Roland's defeat at the Battle of Roncesvalles and his death. Recorded too, is how Saint James appeared in a dream to Charlemagne, urging him to liberate his tomb from the Moors and showing him the route of the Milky Way. This has given the Milky Way and Compostela a figurative relationship associating the starry path of the Milky Way and one of the meanings attributed to the word *Compostela* (*Field of Stars*). Another interpretation of the Milky Way, according to a common medieval legend, is that pilgrims formed the Milky Way from the dust raised by their traveling on the Camino. There is also the Latin word, "composite tella," meaning "burial ground." This makes some sense since a substantial Roman burial ground was found in Santiago. Whatever the source of the name, they are all entertaining and interesting etymological stories.

It is doubtful that Charlemagne ever reached as far west as Santiago or that he ever visited the tomb of Santiago as stated in Book IV of the *Codex*. He could not have liberated the tomb from the Moors because (1) they never possessed it, and (2) the tomb was yet to be discovered. He is credited with being the first pilgrim but that is also doubtful since the tomb was not discovered until 814 and Charlemagne had returned to France long before this, plus he died in January, 814. Thus, it seems valid that many scholars argue that this widely publicized and multi-copied book was a propaganda tool used by the Crown and Catholic Church to drum up recruits for the military Order of Santiago, promote a crusade for the Reconquest of Spain from the Moors, and help popularize the pilgrimage to Santiago.

In brief, the "Chanson de Roland" and Book IV of the *Codex* link Charlemagne to the Camino in multiple ways. While these stories were rooted in embellished historical events, they blossomed into immortalized legends and myths. Some were destined to become great literary works such as the "Chanson de Roland." Some, like the "Chanson," continue to hang out on the Camino and intrigue today's pilgrims much in the same manner as they did in the heyday of the Middle Ages. Pilgrims cannot fail to see the various monuments in Roncesvalles and other towns along the way that recall the feats of the epic hero, Roland and his king.

There are other stories in Book IV that commemorate other parts of the Camino. We shall call on them as we make our way along the Camino. Now it is time to move on to Burguete, our next stop on the Camino, where we find a literary fount of a non-medieval type that has had a profound and perhaps profane influence on the Camino. Read on to the next chapter to find out.

Chapter 2

Meeting Papa Hemingway
and the Gang of Nine

In spite of starting this pilgrimage in the "off season,"
Roncesvalles was very crowded with pilgrims and
tourists. I opted not to stay overnight and instead walked
the extra three kilometers (1.8 miles), commonly called
"klicks," to the town of Burguete and stayed at the Hotel
Burguete, which turned out to be a combination hostel/hotel.
The hostel part was one floor above me and for a while I
thought I might not be able to sleep since it was very noisy
during the early part of the evening. Later things calmed
down and I was able to get a good night's sleep that was so
desperately needed after the trek over the Pyrenees.

Deciding not to stay in Roncesvalles and opting for
Burguete led me to a more modern literary source, for I was
staying in the very hotel that Ernest Hemingway stayed in
when he would go on fishing trips to the Pyrenees. Moreover,
it was also where he wrote his first novel, *The Sun Also Rises*,
in 1926. In the 1920s, Hemingway may not have had any
connection to the Camino, but pilgrims who seek out his hotel

have given him one today. If they can't get a room in the hotel, the very least they do is eat in the hotel's restaurant, where Ernest played the piano and socialized. The old upright piano is still there with his signature. The key cover was locked so I can only assume that it hadn't been played in some time and was probably out of tune.

I tried to recall Hemingway's works. The ones that I remembered best were: *The Old Man and the Sea, For Whom the Bell Tolls,* and *Death in the Afternoon.* The first two became popular as movies as well. I had not read *The Sun Also Rises* so I downloaded it on my iPad and began reading in bed, thinking it might help with my jet lag and make me sleepy; it did. But before I shut off my iPad, the following lines from the novel told me Burguete had changed very little. I saw the same landscape that Hemingway's character Jake saw upon arriving at Burguete: "As we came to the edge of the rise we saw the red roofs and white houses of Burguete ahead…"[1] Burguete still looks the same to today's pilgrims as it did in the 1920s when Hemingway was there.

Hemingway's first novel dealt with what became known as the "lost generation," a generation hung up on itself looking for answers via booze, sex and self-pity. Hemingway would probably be crucified by today's critics for his use of the "N" word and his portrayal of one character, Robert Cohn, as being an outsider to the rest of the characters in the novel because he is a Jew. The other characters often refer to Cohn as a Jew, and once as a "kike." The group avoids him and he is

---

1   Ernest Hemingway, *The Sun Also Rises* (New York: Scribner, 2006 ed.), p. 114.

made unattractive in the novel simply because of being a Jew. It is probably a good thing that this novel is not on the reading list for high school students because the school boards would surely want to ban it on just the presence of the "N" word, like they did a few years ago with Mark Twain's *Huckleberry Finn*. They managed to get Twain's novel published without the "N" word even though it belonged to a part of our history. I cannot fathom why people believe they can change history to suit personal needs.

Hemingway's history in Burguete has still another connection to the Camino. Shopkeepers in the area ply their wares on pilgrims, with souvenirs of both Santiago (Saint James) and Hemingway leading the trade (T-shirts, hats, etc., with their pictures emblazoned on them). Many of the Camino guidebooks mention Hemingway's stays when describing Burguete and Pamplona, along with his favorite hangouts. Somewhat ironic, these two locations (Burguete and Pamplona) have become a pilgrimage within a pilgrimage. Pilgrims will flock to Hemingway's favorite eatery or bar to pay homage or report back home that they stayed where Ernest Hemingway stayed. If Hemingway were alive today, I think he would find it all very amusing as well as a great ego booster.

Upon leaving Burguete I looked back, remembering Hemingway's Jake saying the following while exiting Burguete, almost the same words when he was entering the town: "Looking back we saw Burguete, white houses and red roofs"[2] Looking back I, too, saw those same white houses and red

---

2   Ernest Hemingway, *The Sun Also Rises* (New York: Scribner, 2006 ed.), p. 121.

roofs of the town that Jake saw. That image remains still today and somehow defines the small, lovely town of Burguete.

Hemingway will never be considered an "ugly American" by Spaniards. Yes, there is a lot of controversy and criticism about his ability to speak Spanish and his narrow focus of Spain through bullfighting.[3] No matter what his critics say, at the very least, he brought Spain international fame via his novels, movies made from his novels, writings on bullfighting and his love for their yearly celebration of it in Pamplona. It is said he attended at least seven times. It is also said that Hemingway visited the Spanish writer, Pío Baroja, on his deathbed and stated that he deplored the fact that Baroja had not yet received a Nobel Prize, especially when it was given to so many who deserved it less, like him (Hemingway). According to some critics, Baroja was known not to like Hemingway and his aside remark when he saw Hemingway as an uninvited guest at his deathbed sums up his feelings toward him. He said, "*¿Qué coño hace éste aquí?*"[4] ("*What the hell is this guy doing here?*") (The word *coño* can also mean *cunt*, which would have an even stronger debasement. Take your choice.) It is possible that Hemingway may have gotten wind of this remark or knew of Baroja's feelings toward him since he turned down an offer to be pallbearer at Baroja's funeral, but that is only speculation. Moreover, another critic states that Hemingway declined the pallbearer invitation "…saying that

---

3   Jeffrey Herlihy-Mera, "'*He Was Sort of a Joke, In Fact*': Ernest Hemingway in Spain," *The Hemingway Review*, Vol. 31, No. 2 (Moscow, Idaho: University of Idaho, 2012), pp. 1–22.

4   Herlihy-Mera, p. 9.

it was an honor that should be reserved for Spaniards."[5]

Even though Hemingway has been dead for over fifty years, Spaniards carry on his legend to this day. We will see more of this attitude when we get to Pamplona, where his legend becomes a pilgrimage within a pilgrimage.

Continuing my trek I passed several villages during the day. Just about 18.9 klicks (11.3 miles) from Burguete, I encountered a bridge called *Puente de la Rabia* (*Bridge of Rabies* or *Rabies' Bridge*). Now, with a name like that there just has to be a story connected to it. And, of course, there is.

Let me begin it by describing the bridge itself. It is an ancient Gothic stone bridge. The bridge, with its center pier and twin arches, crosses the Arga River into the little town of Zubiri. (*Zubiri* in the Basque language means *village of the bridge*.) As with many legends there are many versions and this one concerning the bridge is no exception. There's a Portuguese and a French version. The one I am reporting on centers in Spain and concerns a much-venerated fifth century Christian martyr by the name of Saint Quiteria. According to legend, Saint Quiteria was one of nine sisters all born at the same time. The nine girls' mother was a lady of high rank and she was outraged that she had given birth to nine children like a common animal, and even more so, that she had nine daughters and no son. In a fit of rage, she demanded that her nurse take the babies and drown them in the river. The nurse could not do it so she took them to a remote village where the girls grew up together. Then things

5   Douglas Edward LaPrade, *Hemingway and Franco* (Valencia: Universitat de Valencia, 2007), p. 115.

really went haywire. They formed a warrior gang of nine.

The girls were all good Christians and their gang was formed to travel around breaking Christians out of jail. They spent a number of years doing this until they were caught and returned to their father, a Galician prince, who recognized them merely from family resemblance. He told them all to marry good Roman pagans but they refused and broke out of jail. They waged guerilla warfare against the Roman Empire. Eventually, the girls were all killed or died. Quiteria was beheaded by her father because she refused to renounce her Christianity and marry a pagan. (Her father imparts new meaning to parental abuse and punishment. He was probably not named "father of the year.")

It is also reported that Quiteria held at bay two mad rabid dogs with her saintly voice, and is often invoked in prayer to help in the prevention or cure of rabies. She is depicted in paintings and sculpture always leading a dog. It turns out that some—or maybe all—of Saint Quiteria's relics are embedded in the central pier of the bridge. So, for over a thousand years—and still to this very day—local farmers believe that if they march their animals three times over the central pier of the bridge, the animal will be immune from rabies. Also, they believe that if they walk a rabies-infected animal three times around the central pier (the river in the summer is not all that deep) that it will be cured of the disease! Talk about faith! I am sure the animals are most appreciative of this preventive measure, since it means avoiding a shot from the vet and no possible side effects.

But wait there is still more to Quiteria's story. During the Middle Ages the bridge was undergoing some repairs.

Workers discovered bones buried beneath one of the bridge's pillars and attributed them to Quiteria (nobody's sure how they managed to connect them to her but they did). The workers took these "relics" to the local church and they were given a place of honor. However, the next day the townspeople discovered the relics had disappeared. They were soon rediscovered back beneath the bridge. The people thought this was a sign that Saint Quiteria wished to remain at the bridge, so that is where her bones have remained. And now you know the rest of the story.

On I trekked past the towns of Zubiri and Larrasoaña to arrive at a charming *Casa Rural* (*Bed and Breakfast*) called Akerreta. It is in a very isolated location but still directly on the Camino. This establishment can claim some fame since a scene from the movie, *The Way*, was shot here in 2010. If you see the movie, look for Martin Sheen having a discussion with the female Canadian pilgrim on the patio of this lodging.

Having booked a room in this lodging I spent a most restful night and a lovely breakfast before departing. With the sun well up, I started on my way. At the end of the day I would meet up with Ernest Hemingway again, this time in Pamplona.

Chapter 3

Legendary Personae

About fourteen klicks from the B&B, Akerreta, I encountered the first major city on the French route of the Camino, Pamplona. Its international renown only came at the penning of Hemingway's novel, *The Sun Also Rises,* and his numerous attendances at the San Fermin Festival. He details the "running of the bulls" during the month of July and the feast of San Fermin in this novel. Since its publication and popularity, tourists have crowded into the city to partake in the bacchanalian revelry and observe the annual rite of the "running of the bulls." This was another reason I chose not to do my trek during the month of July, since it would be overcrowded and difficult to get inexpensive lodging and food. (Travel Tip #4: Always check for local festivals and national holidays or celebrations to avoid crowds and higher costs.)

I was familiar with some of Hemingway's other hangouts (Madrid and Key West, Florida, in particular), having lived in both places for extended periods of time. Pamplona was new to me. I knew there were walking tours that focused on his "watering holes" and even a tour of the room where he stayed while in Pamplona. I did not want to be pressed into a group of tourists so I set out on my own pilgrimage within a pilgrimage to see if I could comprehend this man's love for a country and its traditions that were not his. He not only exposed his love through his artistic work but also through his residency in the country itself. Unlike most Americans he became steeped in the culture and language. He showed a deep appreciation for both. These are visible in his work and his daily life. Just a quick visit to some of his frequented spots and their counterparts in his novel reveal how interrelated nonfiction and fiction are in the novel.

One of the places was the Gran Hotel La Perla, where he stayed when in Pamplona. In his novel it is called the Hotel Montoya. La Perla was recently renovated and is rated as a five-star hotel. Room 201 is Hemingway's room, complete with the original furniture. In the novel it was room 217. La Perla is located on the Plaza de Castillo in the heart of the city, as was the Montoya of the novel. From the hotel it is a few steps across the plaza to the Café Iruña, which Hemingway frequented all too often. In his novel, we get a good description of the café: "We went down the stairs and out the door and walked across the square toward the Café Iruña…Across the square the white wicker tables and chairs of the Iruña extended out beyond the Arcade to the edge of the street."[1] And again on the day of the feast of San Fermin, he goes to the café, where: "The marble-topped tables and white wicker chairs were gone. They were replaced by cast-iron

---

1   Hemingway, p.138.

tables and severe folding chairs. The café was like a battleship stripped for action."[2]

While the café remains located in the same spot described in the novel, and the terraced sitting area is familiar, the inside of the café has taken on the likings of a sanctuary dedicated to his "holiness Hemingway." There is a lifelike statue of Hemingway standing at the bar and it is aptly named, "Hemingway's Corner."

Just a short ways away and almost parallel to *Plaza Castillo* (*Castle* Square) are *Plaza Consistorial* (*Town Council* Square) and the Town Hall, the latter with its magnificent façade that combines artistic features from both baroque and neoclassical periods. The building's façade never fails to elicit "oohs" and "ahs" from newcomers to the city. The *Ayuntamiento* (*Town Hall*) appears to be the same today as it did in *The Sun Also Rises*. Hemingway's description in the novel could just as well have described the photo taken by me in 2013 (see photos): "The three of us walked along, past the Ayuntamiento the banners hung from the balcony,..."[3] And later when the mark of the fiesta begins: "Before the waiter brought the sherry, the rocket that announced the fiesta went up in the square. It burst and there was a gray ball of smoke high up above... another rocket came up to it, trickling smoke in the bright sunlight."[4]

Nothing has changed with the start of the festivities. Someone still fires the rocket at the Town Hall to signal the start of the week-long celebration and the running of the

---

2   Ibid., p. 157.

3   Ibid., pp. 141–2.

4   Ibid., p. 157.

bulls as was done in *The Sun Also Rises*. Whether Hemingway inspired the non-stop drinking and partying atmosphere of San Fermin week or it inspired him to drink remains a moot question. However, there is no question he had a profound and profane effect on Pamplona and its rise to fame. Critics can deride Hemingway's presence in Spain and scoff at what they term his narrow focus on Spanish culture, that is, bullfighting, but you can bet the merchants and hotel owners are laughing all the way to the bank when the hordes of Hemingway fans show up every July for the annual celebration that he fostered and advanced throughout the world.

In spite of what critics say about his narrow focus on Spanish culture, Hemingway was very knowledgeable about Spain's literature. He often refers to classic Spanish works of literature and uses them in his works to unify a common idea or ideal. In his novel that deals with the Spanish Civil War, *For Whom the Bell Tolls*, he links the killing of a man by a mob of villagers in Lope de Vega's drama, *Fuenteovejuna,* to the Republicans' participation in a mass slaying of Fascists in the civil war. Not only does Hemingway bring classical Spanish literature into this novel by means of Lope de Vega, he also links this novel to other authors of Spain's Golden Age, such as Cervantes, Quevedo, and Calderón. As one critic says, "Hemingway makes a deliberate effort to invoke the Renaissance in Spain, just as the same novel alludes to Spain's earlier historical eras."[5]

Hemingway is not the only person of influence in this festivity. After all it is also a religious celebration in honor of

---

5   LaPrade, p. 48.

San Fermin, a co-patron of Navarre, along with Saint Francis Xavier. San Fermin is honored with a religious procession. His statue is carried aloft through the streets followed by bands playing traditional music. Why San Fermin is connected to the running of the bulls is somewhat ironic. He was martyred in France, not torn apart by being tied to wild bulls as the popular legend has it, but beheaded. The bull honor goes to his predecessor, San Saturninus, who was tied to a bull and dragged to his death. San Saturninus did baptize San Fermin and sent him to preach throughout Navarre. San Fermin eventually returned to Pamplona to become its first bishop. Attributing his death to being dragged by bulls makes for a convenient link to the running of the bulls and provides a legitimate excuse for celebrating.

In addition to the stories of San Fermin and Hemingway, the *Codex* once again makes another appearance with its recording of Charlemagne's destruction of Pamplona and the telling of one of Saint James's miracles that took place in Pamplona. Let's start first with Charlemagne's presence in Pamplona.

According to Book IV of the *Codex*, also known as the *Pseudo-Turpin* (referred to as *PT* from here on in this book), Charlemagne's first victory in Spain was the defeat and destruction of Pamplona. At that time the city was surrounded by high, thick walls, so the victory was not an overnight success. You just might see a slight resemblance to the Battle of Jericho. In Chapter IV of *PT*, we read:

The first city besieged is Pamplona. For three months its mighty walls hold out. Then Charlemagne prays to the Lord and Saint James to help him. The walls crumble. The Emperor spares such Saracens as will be baptized and slays the rest. Other Saracens, when they hear this, surrender themselves and their cities and give tribute to Charlemagne, the whole land is laid under tribute.[6]

While most historians refute that the walls were destroyed in this manner (there is still a large section of the medieval wall remaining today), they do agree that Charlemagne probably did destroy the gates by having them burned. At any rate, Charlemagne does leave his mark on Pamplona and it returns to haunt him at the Battle of Roncesvalles, for it was there that the Basques received retribution for the destruction Charlemagne inflicted upon them at Pamplona and many of their other towns and villages.

For more lore that takes place in Pamplona we turn to Book II of the *Codex*, which contains the miracles of Saint James. The specific miracle that focuses on Pamplona is number six, entitled, "A Story of Saint James Written Down By His Excellency Pope Calixtus." In brief, it is the story of a man who sets out with his wife and two small children for the shrine at Santiago. They arrive at Pamplona and his wife dies in the inn where they are staying. The innkeeper takes all the man's property, including his money and his horse. We are never told that these things were taken to cover expenses, such as the wife's burial, but that they were taken in a wicked way. Nevertheless, the man continues on the pilgrimage carrying his children in his arms. Unknowingly, he encounters Saint James along the way and relates his tale of woe. Saint James

---

6   H.W. Smyser, *The Pseudo-Turpin* (Cambridge, MA, The Mediaeval Academy of America, Publication No. 30, 1937), p. 18. (All future quotes from the *Pseudo-Turpin* will be taken from Smyser's edition.)

offers his best donkey to him with the provision he return it to him in Santiago, since that is where he resides. Once the man arrives in Santiago he goes to pray at the shrine. Saint James appears to him wearing very bright clothing and says:

"Don't you know me, brother?"

The pilgrim responded, "Not at all, my lord."

To this the other responded, "I am the apostle of Christ who in the region of Pamplona supplied you with my donkey when you were in such grief. Now, however, I am supplying you with the donkey from now until you have returned to your own area, and I am announcing to you that your wicked innkeeper in Pamplona is about to fall headfirst from his seat and die from this serious fall, because he took your goods unjustly.[7]

The pilgrim returns to Pamplona and finds the innkeeper quite dead, having fallen from his chair and broken his neck. The story ends with an admonishment of evil innkeepers along with a formulaic topos found in almost all the miracles in Book II, except for numbers 8, 16, 17 and 18: "This was accomplished by the Lord and it is miraculous in our eyes."[8] As for the admonishment:

Therefore it is plainly shown in this miracle that all crafty innkeepers are condemned to eternal death if they unjustly take the inventory of a guest, whether living or dead, which should be given to the churches and the poor of Christ as alms for the redemption of souls.[9]

---

7   Coffey et al., p. 71.

8   Ibid.

9   Ibid., p. 72.

In addition to this miracle being recorded in the *Codex*, it is also immortalized in a Renaissance retablo (elaborately carved altarpiece that is a backdrop for the altar). This one is in the Monastery of Santiago in Pamplona and shows Saint James appearing to the pilgrim and his two children after the death of his wife and after being robbed of all their possessions by the evil innkeeper. They are walking on the Camino and Saint James is shown giving them a donkey so they can continue their pilgrimage. Above the scene is a script held by angels that contains a description that identifies the legend.

The admonishment of evil innkeepers and warnings to pilgrims about them are prevalent themes in the *Codex*. It begins in the letter attributed to Pope Calixtus that prefaces Book I (remember, he is no longer accepted as the author; however, his name is used as a promotional tool and to lend authenticity in that time period). The pseudo pope-author relates that Christ appears along with Saint James and urges him not to delay in "… correcting the evils of the depraved innkeepers dwelling on the route of my apostle."[10] The author does just that in Book I, chapter 17 in the sermon titled, "Veneranda Dies" ("Day to be Honored"). He rants at length in an exposition of the iniquity of innkeepers, giving caveats to the pilgrim. Here is a sampling:

But what shall I say about evil innkeepers, who deceive pilgrims with so many frauds? Just as Judas received the punishment for his guilt from the Lord Jesus Christ in His passion, and just as the thief received his reward for his confession, the evil innkeepers will also receive punishments in hell for their iniquities on the route of Saint

---

10   Ibid., p. 4.

James, and the truthful pilgrims are to receive the rewards of their good works and their hardships in heaven. Therefore the evil innkeepers on the route of Saint James are damned for violating pilgrims with countless frauds. Some, in fact go out to meet them at the gateways of the villages, kissing them as if they were their relatives coming from faraway regions. What more do they do? Leading them into their homes, they promise them all sorts of good things and do evil things. Whom shall I say they are like, except the traitor Judas who betrayed the Lord by kissing Him?[11]

We shall hear later on the Camino, a story of an innkeeper's evil daughter (I guess it runs in the family as a genetic defect), but that is for further down the road.

In the interim, there are a couple of stories still to do with Pamplona. One story concerns the patroness of Pamplona, *La Virgen del Camino* (*The Virgin of the Way*). According to legend, the statue of this patroness was originally in a small chapel in the village of Alfaro. It mysteriously appeared one day in 1487 on a roof beam of the San Cernín church (also known as San Saturnino) in Pamplona. Villagers tried for two years to return the statue to their chapel, but each night it returned to Pamplona. It now resides in the beautiful and spacious single-nave church of San Cernín, in a baroque-style chapel. Her official title is "Lady and Queen of the City."

About 4.5 klicks (2.7 miles) outside Pamplona heading toward Santiago is allegedly the location where Charlemagne finally defeats Aigolandus, the leader of the Saracens. After several evasions made by Aigolandus, Charlemagne finally manages to confront and defeat him. Most of the events

---

11 Ibid., p. 34.

surrounding his defeat are in *PT*, chapters XIV–XVIII of Smyser's translation. Here is a summary of those events from these chapters: Charlemagne demands that Aigolandus give up the city. The Saracen decides to fight instead, but before he does he asks for a truce in order to meet with Charlemagne. In the interim, he brings his army out from Pamplona and faces Charlemagne's army along the Camino. The commanders begin their conference and to Aigolandus's surprise and delight, Charlemagne speaks to him in Arabic. We are told that he learned it as a boy while living in Toledo for a short time. Aigolandus questions Charlemagne's right to claim Spain and he answers that Christians have been chosen to rule the world by Christ. Aigolandus refuses to believe this and will not accept baptism. Both agree they must fight to determine which faith is the true faith. Aigolandus agrees to submit to baptism if he loses and is allowed to live.

The battle ensues and the Saracens are soundly defeated. Aigolandus promises that he and his people will accept baptism the next day. The next day, Aigolandus returns and here is why he does not convert:

…Aigolandus finds Charles (anglicized name for Charlemagne used by translator) at table surrounded by religious [people] in various vestments.

He inquires as to the meaning of the vestments and is told that such and such habits denote bishops and priests, such and such denote monks, canons regular, and so forth. Meanwhile, however, he spies twelve paupers, segregated from the other diners. Very poorly clad, and seated on the ground without table or cloths, they are supplied but sparingly with food and drink. He is told that these are messengers of God to the number of the apostles; Charles provides for them for the sake of our Lord. Aigolandus resents the fact that

Charles entertains his religious, his own vassals, far better than "God's messengers;" he decides forthwith that Christianity is no true faith and announces that he will not be baptized.[12]

The battle takes place the following day and Charlemagne slays Aigolandus with only a few of the Saracens getting away. However, there is a moral tone inserted into the event by the fact that Charlemagne knows that his lack of charity to his "messengers of God" has resulted in the loss of converts to Christianity. The author states, "Let this be a lesson to all Christians to be ever mindful of the needy."[13]

The Christian moral is heard again when some of the Christians return to the battlefield the next night and strip the dead bodies of anything of value. While loaded with their booty, the Saracens are able to ride in and slay them with little difficulty. The author says, "These Christians are like some religious who having conquered vice, return to vice and thus lose eternal life."[14] While Charlemagne may have won this battle, the war is far from over, as we shall see later on the Camino. So on we go to the next lore on the Camino.

The next story takes place near the peak of *Alto del Perdón*. You've heard of Pike's Peak, well this is *Pardon's Peak* or better said, *Forgiveness Peak*. Before reaching the summit or peak, there is a dried up fountain where the legend, "Fuente Reniega" ("Fountain of Renouncement" or "Denial") occurred. This legend concerns a pilgrim traveling

---

12   Smyser, p. 30.

13   Ibid.

14   Ibid.

the Camino, who is thirsty and exhausted from his walk. He meets a fellow traveler who turns out to be the Devil in disguise. The Devil offers to show the pilgrim a hidden source of water but only on the condition that he renounces God, the Virgin Mary and Saint James. The pilgrim holds steadfast to his faith even though he is near dying from lack of water. He refuses to do what this man asks. The Devil leaves and the man prepares himself for death. At that moment Saint James, also disguised as a pilgrim, appears and leads the thirsty and exhausted man to a rock. Using a scallop shell (a symbol associated with Saint James), Saint James strikes the rock and provides the traveler with water to quench his thirst. The fountain can still be seen today, but it no longer is functioning as a source of potable water.

Walking onwards and upwards along the path, Alto Del Perdón comes in to view, where there is a gigantic but lifelike metal sculpture of twelve pilgrims. They almost seem like paper doll cutouts strung across the peak. Some are on foot and others on horseback. There is a stone inscription that reads, "Donde se cruza el camino del viento con el de las estrellas" ("Where the path of the wind crosses that of the stars"). The piece is by Navarre sculptor, Vicente Galbete, and was done in 1996.

The sculpture exhibits a small history of pilgrims and the pilgrimage. It represents both the pilgrim and the pilgrimage through various stages of development, that is, from the beginning in the Middle Ages up to the present day in the form of a procession. Of the twelve pilgrims, the first pilgrim appears to be searching for the route and symbolizes the beginning of interest in the pilgrimage. Next is a group of three that depict the growth or rise in popularity of the Camino. These three are followed by another group depicted as merchants or tradesmen on horseback that symbolize the medieval era of merchants hawking their wares to the pilgrims. Spaced away from them is a solitary figure that characterizes the decline in pilgrimages due to political, religious and social unrests from the mid-fourteenth to the mid-twentieth centuries. At the very end of the procession are two modern-day figures depicted to show the renewed interest and rise in popularity in the pilgrimage in the late twentieth century. It is a gigantic piece of sculpture befitting the vista. Its location offers an ideal rest spot to the weary pilgrim after his/ her tiring ascent to the peak. In addition, this place allows the pilgrim a period of reflection while contemplating both the piece of art and the view.

Now we plod on to Óbanos, a small but famous village during the medieval period. Its location at the junction of the two main routes to Santiago was a resting place for pilgrims. While Óbanos appears to be a quiet, peaceful village it does have a rather notorious past, which leads us to the legend of San Guillén and Santa Felicia.

Felicia was the sister of Guillén of Aquitaine who, following the family tradition, decided to embark on a pilgrimage to Santiago. Upon returning from Santiago, she finds life at Court unsuitable for her due to the profound experiences received from the pilgrimage. She decides to help those less fortunate than herself, so she leaves the French court and heads back to Navarra to live as a recluse and servant.

Her family is not pleased and they send her brother, Guillén, to try to bring her back. After much searching Guillén finally tracks her down to the village of Óbanos, but despite much begging and pleading Felicia refuses to return to France with her brother. He becomes so angry with her that in a fit of rage he stabs and kills his sister with a dagger. (No anger management classes back then.)

Guillén, aggrieved with guilt and remorse, decides as atonement he will make a pilgrimage to Santiago. Once he reaches Santiago he realizes why his sister felt the way she did and he, too, decides to dedicate his life helping others. He returns to Óbanos and builds the shrine called, *Nuestra Señora de Arnotegui*. He lives out his days helping pilgrims and dedicating his life to prayer. Both he and his sister were canonized.

The meaning of the Basque word "Arnotegui" is not clear but etymologists claim it means "vineyard," "vine," "wine cellar," and/or "eagle." The more appropriate translation of *Nuestra Señora de Arnotegui* might be *Our Lady of the Vineyard* (or *Vine*), since her statue shows her holding grapes. No matter what the correct translation might be, it doesn't seem to matter to her followers. What is more noteworthy is that a passion play was created from the story of these two siblings (Guillén and Felicia). Since 1965 performances have taken place in the town square of Óbanos. Known as the *Misterio de Óbanos* (*Mystery of Óbanos*), the play is now staged every two years in July and more than six hundred actors take part. The *Misterio de Óbanos* has been declared a "Fiesta of National Tourist Interest."

Another side note on this story is that Santa Felicia's grave is in Labiano, a tiny village not far from Pamplona, where villagers believe that by venerating her remains they will be cured of their headaches. San Guillén's relics can be found in the shrine, Nuestra Señora de Arnotegui, and every Holy Thursday his silver-covered skull is used to bless the wine that is given to the villagers.

Our next town of importance is *Puente la Reina* (*The Queen's Bridge*). The town is famous for its Romanesque bridge. This bridge was built over the river Arga in the eleventh century, at the insistence of a queen, who could well have been Doña Mayor de Castilla, the wife of Sancho el Mayor. It is considered one of the most majestic examples of Romanesque architecture on the Camino. Its most notable features are its six semi-circular arches. The aim of its construction was twofold: it made it easier for pilgrims on the Road to Santiago to leave the town after going along the *Rúa Mayor* (*Main Street*) and easier for the merchants and tradesmen to attract business.

The bridge used to have three defensive towers, one at each end and a central one, which housed the Renaissance image of the *Virgen del Puy*, also known as the *Txori* (a Basque word for "bird"). The legend associated with this bridge and statue of the Virgin tells us that the statue used to be visited by a little bird that looked after it and groomed it. The bird would remove cobwebs with its wings and wash its face with water it collected from the river Arga. It is said that whenever the txori appeared, the church bells would begin to ring. In David M. Gitlitz and Linda Kay Davidson's *The Pilgrimage Road to Santiago*, the following is reported:

In 1825, 1834, 1840, and 1842–43, a strange lark (locally, a txori) used to fly around and around the statue of the Virgin. Bells began to ring by themselves. When local worshipers approached in procession, their joyous noise did not scare off the bird. In 1834 General Viamanuel laughed at the miracle and forbade the celebration of the txori, which he had put in a cage. Shortly afterward, he was taken prisoner in one of the battles of the Carlist Wars.[15]

If you visit the bridge today you will no longer find the image of the Virgin Mary, as it was moved to the church of San Pedro, close to the river, in 1843.

Upon leaving Puente la Reina for Santiago, pilgrims cross its famous bridge marked with a yellow arrow showing them that they are going in the right direction. The yellow arrows and the scallop shells found along the Camino were put there fairly recently, mainly through the work of Father D. Elias Valiña Sampedro. His tireless efforts from the 1960s to his death in 1989 revived the Santiago pilgrimages and made navigation for the pilgrim much easier and safer. Of course, there is a story connected to his work of placing the markers and this is how it goes.

Before Spain joined the European Union they had border guards and patrols along the borders between Spain and France. One day, Father Sampedro was near the border painting the yellow arrow markers on some boulders and fences. Border guards saw him and asked him what he was doing. His reply was something like, "I am preparing for an invasion!" Well, you can image what turmoil that caused. The guards hauled the priest away for questioning. After they found out what he really meant by his reply they released him. And as they say, "the rest is history!"

---

15   David M. Gitlitz and Linda Kay Davidson, *The Pilgrimage Road to Santiago* (New York: St. Martin's Griffin, 2000), p. 88.

Chapter 4

Legends of the Scallop Shell and the Oca

As mentioned in the previous chapter, the scallop shell is used as a marker to show the way to Santiago. It was also the customary symbol worn by medieval pilgrims who completed the pilgrimage to Santiago. Wearing a symbol is and always has been quite common among pilgrims. Pilgrims in Rome carried a replica of the keys of Saint Peter and in Jerusalem they carried palm fronds. The scallop shell became connected with the pilgrimage to Santiago during the Middle Ages. It was like a badge that had a twofold purpose. One was to show that the person who displayed it was a pilgrim and should be treated accordingly, that is, with respect and care, as stated in Book V, chapter XI of the *Codex*. Those who did otherwise received some form of retribution from God and/or Saint James. For example, there is the story of a pilgrim who begged for some bread from a village woman in the name of God and Saint James. The village woman had some bread baking on the hearth but told the pilgrim there was none. When the pilgrim heard that there was no bread, the pilgrim shouted, "May the bread you have turn into stone!"[1] And of course it did. Moral of this story: Don't mess with pilgrims!

The other historical purpose of the scallop shell was to show that the pilgrim had completed the pilgrimage. It became a badge of honor for the pilgrim. Wearing the shell on the return trip home accorded the pilgrims more respect and honor since they had achieved a tremendous spiritual goal in a very perilous environment. In the Middle Ages, the pilgrim would probably pick up his shell after he reached Santiago, and most likely at Finisterre. However, it is recorded in Book V of the *Codex* that scallop shells were sold at the entrance to the cathedral by 1150. By the thirteenth century the selling of the shell became regulated and there were one hundred scallop shell vendors in Santiago.

The shape of the scallop shell lends itself to metaphorical interpretations. The routes that pilgrims traveled to Santiago are represented by the grooves on the shell. These different grooves or routes join together at a single point where the two halves of the shell are permanently joined. This joining point represents the common destination of the pilgrims: the tomb of Saint James.

On a higher plane, the shell represents life's journey and the final stop before reaching paradise. In times past, most pilgrims picked up their scallop shells at Finisterre since they were so plentiful there along the shores and because the place itself was symbolic. Celts, Romans and Christians revered this place—either out of fear or a belief that it was a stepping stone to the afterlife.

_____

1   William Melczer, *The Pilgrim's Guide to Santiago de Compostela* (New York: Italica Press, 1993) pp. 132–33.

The Celts believed their god of the underworld, Dis, inhabited this place, so it was here they held rites pertaining to death. They believed Finisterre was the lowest coast, the place where souls of the dead gathered to follow the sun across the sea. The *Altar Soli* (*Sun Altar*) of the Celts was also here, and they engaged in sun idolatry and fertility rituals.

The Romans had their opinion, too. They would sit and watch the sunset and swear they could hear the hissing sounds as the fiery sun sank into the ocean. (My opinion is that they had too much wine at "happy hour.")

Christians saw it as the last stop of the journey in earthly life. To reach Finisterre was a mystical transformation for the pilgrim. He had completed the earthly journey to the ends of the earth. His next journey would be to the afterlife and then, hopefully, to heaven. Legend assigns this path to the ends of the earth as a place where Celts, Romans and Christians walked as they approached their time of death, many of which, died along the way. Today it is not uncommon to see special markings or areas of remembrance built along the Camino to honor those who have died while making the pilgrimage. One that was done for a cyclist lies just outside the tiny village of Acebo, near the local cemetery. This is a monument erected in memory of a German cyclist who died there in 1987 on his way to Santiago de Compostela. The monument shows his bike atop a gigantic boulder. Other memorials such as white crosses or piles of stone marked with a name and date are often seen along the path or roadside.

Pilgrims today still wear the shell but it is no longer proof that the person wearing it completed the journey. You can buy them worldwide. Today's pilgrim carries a *credencial* (a type of passport that is stamped, signed and dated wherever the pilgrim stops to eat or stay for the night). Many of the stamps have the shell symbol incorporated in the logo. This document is inspected at the Pilgrim's Office in Santiago and if it meets the standards for completing the pilgrimage, the bearer is issued a *Compostela* (a certificate written in Latin that states the person whose name appears on it is recognized as having completed the pilgrimage).

Wearing the scallop shell dates back to the eleventh century when Spain was in the throes of the Reconquista, or the taking back of lands held by the invading Moors. One reason given for choosing the scallop shell as a symbol for Saint James comes from multiple legends. According to one tale, when Saint James was unearthed, he was found covered in scallop shells. Another legend has it that during the transport of Saint James's body from Palestine to Galicia via boat there was a terrible storm and his body was lost at sea. After some time the body washed ashore on the Galician coast undamaged, but covered in scallop shells.

Yet another legend has it that Saint James's boat approached the Galician shore where a wedding was taking place. The bridegroom's horse spooked. Horse and rider plunged into the sea and appeared to be drowning. However, through Saint James's aid they were saved. Both horse and rider emerged from the depths covered in scallop shells.

Another version of the previous legend states that the bridegroom was riding to meet the wedding party. His horse lost its footing on a rocky cliff and both fell into the depths below. The ending, however, is the same. Saint James saves them and both emerge from the sea covered in scallop shells.

One of the miracles of Saint James recorded in the *Codex* is directly linked to the scallop shell. In Miracle 12, we read of a soldier who "…became swollen in the throat region as a sack full of air." The soldier could find no remedy for his condition, so he turned to Saint James. The soldier had great faith in Saint James and he knew the scallop shell was Saint James's icon. He believed that if he found a scallop shell he would only have to touch it to his throat and he would be cured. He found one on a pilgrim who happened to be his neighbor. He touched the shell to his throat and was immediately cured. He then set out for Santiago to give thanks for his cure.

Again in the sermon found in the *Codex*, Book I, chapter 17 titled, "Veneranda Dies", there is a detailed explanation of the scallop shell regarding its name in other languages and its use by pilgrims:

There are some fish in the sea of Blessed James, which the people call veras, having two shields, one on either side, between which the fish is covered as if between two shells in the likeness of an oyster. These shells, of course, are shaped like the fingers of a hand, and the Provençals call them nidulas and the French call them crusillas, and the pilgrims returning from the threshold of Blessed James sew them on their capes, and they wear them back to their own country with great exultation in honor of the apostle and in his memory and a sign of such a great journey.[2]

Then the author goes on to describe how the shell represents the values and duties of a Christian and what the shell symbolizes when those duties are performed, including the final reward for pursuing them. The rationalization in the following passage is somewhat extreme but should provide

2   Davidson et al., p.25.

some humor for dedicated logicians. The author writes:

Therefore, the two shields with which the fish is protected, one on either side, represent the two laws of charity with which the bearer must truly protect his life: that is, to love God above all things and to love one's neighbor as oneself. A person who loves God is one who keeps his commandments. A person who loves one's neighbor as one loves oneself is one who does not do to anyone else what he does not want done to himself and who does to others what he would justly want done for himself. The shields, however, which are modified in the shape of fingers, signify good works in which the bearer of this sign must persevere; and good works are beautifully signified by fingers, since we work through them when we do something. Therefore, just as the pilgrim bears the shell as long as he is in the course of this present life, he must also carry the yoke of the Lord, that is, submit to His commandments. And it is truly right and just that one who has sought such a great apostle and such a great man in such a remote region in toil and hardship persevere in good works to the extent that he may receive with Saint James the crown in the heavenly land.[3]

Even though pilgrims to Santiago connected to Saint James through the scallop shell, the scallop shell had been used as a religious symbol and an artistic device long before the pilgrim started wearing and popularizing it as a symbol for doing and completing the pilgrimage to Santiago. Early Christian artworks in the catacombs depict figures using the scallop shell as a container for the baptismal water. Early baptismal fonts are in the shape of a scallop shell. Pilgrims on the Camino see not only the scallop shell as directional markers, but also see it on the many architectural structures as a decorous design. They see it on church pillars, domes,

---

3   Ibid., pp.25–6.

apses, emblems, plaza monuments, and business signs, to
name a few.

One of the most memorable monuments on the Camino
that is decorated with the scallop shell is found in the small
hamlet of Boadilla del Camino. The town, in the fifteenth
century in celebration of its independence from the Lords
of Melgar and Castrogeriz, erected a gibbet so they could
hang their own local criminals without interference from
nobility. This gibbet in Spanish is called a *rollo jurisdiccional*,
which does not translate easily into English. Think of it as
an ornate stone column that represented the administering
of justice by the local town council. In other words, it was
a symbol for having judicial power. There are still a few of
these monuments left in Spain and the one in Boadilla is quite
ornate. It has weathered the centuries quite well. The rollo
was not only used for hanging criminals but also to humiliate
offenders before bringing them to trial by chaining them to
the pillar and putting them on public display.

In brief, the scallop shell's origin and function were
multiple. It had practical uses as well as spiritual or religious
ones. Used as a container, one could scoop water for
drinking or use it as a dish for food. The sharp edges could
serve as a digging tool. Surrounded by myth and legend, it
still continues to be a bit mysterious and evades a definite,
clear meaning. Its association with Celtic fertility rites and
its use as a symbol for a rising and setting sun (birth and
death), almost coincides with similar Roman beliefs on birth
and death. For them, the scallop shell signified the birth of
Venus from the sea. But no matter what the connection of
the scallop shell was among the early travelers of this road,

pilgrims still continue to display or wear it.

In walking the Camino, I could not help but notice the number of places that had the name *Oca* (*Goose*) associated with them. Oca is the feminine form and, believe it or not, in all fairness to the genders, there is a town called *El Ganso* on the Camino, which also means "goose" but of the masculine gender (referred to as the "gander" in English). Another place name along the Camino referring to "goose" is: *Montes de Oca* (*Hills of the Goose*). The word *Villafranca* was added to *Montes de Oca* and translates as *Town of the Franks* (the origin of the name was due to the fact that many foreigners settled there). Another translation given is *Freetown*, because the inhabitants were released from paying feudal taxes. *French Town* was yet another interpretation because so many French merchants and artists made their way to these areas and ended up becoming permanent or semi-permanent residents.

Other place names referring to the goose are aptly summarized by Mercedes C. Quesada-Embid in her doctoral dissertation titled, *"Dwelling, Walking, Serving: Organic Preservation Along the Camino de Santiago Pilgrimage Landscape."* Here is her summary of the place names:

In the region of La Rioja there are toponyms of towns and areas surrounding the Camino with the names: Ocón (large goose), Ojacastro (Castros are Celtic fortified settlements, this one is called the Celtic settlement of the Goose), and Oja River (old Spanish variation of the term Oca). As well as to the north of the route there are names such as: Oco (male goose) found to the east of the town of Estella, Ocáriz, Oquina (female goose adjective), Ocilla or Oquilla (Small Female Goose), Ocarazo (large male goose), Peña Oqueta (Goose-like Mountain), Oca, Nanclares de Oca, Leciñana de Oca, Villanueva de la Oca (New village of the Goose), River Oca with the town of Zugastieta y Oca on its shores…These are all different ways of saying the word goose.[4]

What is more interesting is that Quesada-Embid states that the Camino de Santiago in "legends unveil that the route used to have the name *Camino de las Ocas Salvajes* or *Way of the Wild Geese*.[5] Pilgrims can still see the goose sign (footprint of a goose) on the Camino and what is surprising is that it is similar to the scallop shell, except it has fewer lines radiating from its central point. It looks similar to a trident, or like the following symbol: Ψ. One of the clearest representations of this symbol is to be found at *Puente la Reina* (*Queen's Bridge*), a small town encountered previously in this book. Here in the *Iglesia del Crucificado* (*Church of the Crucifixion*) the image of Christ is on a cross that is clearly shaped like the foot of a goose. However, I had to satisfy my curiosity for the goose sign since its name appeared so frequently along the Camino. So I probed deeper into the matter.

Upon further investigation I discovered that geese were once sacred guides sent to advise humanity and also sentinels used to warn the farmer of any intruder on his property. Because of their migratory habits, they established fixed routes, one of which just happened to coincide with the Camino. Because pilgrims did not have maps, their only navigational tools were questioning residents along the way, the stars at night and those migratory flocks of geese that

---

4   Mercedes C. Quesada-Embid, *"Dwelling, Walking, Serving: Organic Preservation Along the Camino de Santiago Pilgrimage Landscape"* (Antioch University New England, 2008), p.86.

5   Ibid., p. 87.

flew the Camino during the day. As time passed, a game was developed called *El juego de la Oca* (*Goose Game* or *Game of the Goose*). Some attribute the invention of this game to the Knights Templar and others to master architects along the Camino, but no one knows for sure. More speculation is that it was not only a game, but also an encoded guide to Santiago de Compostela. It was a board game with sixty-three numbered spaces shaped to form a maze or labyrinth. Many of the spaces have images of the goose, hence its name. The game also represented the different stages of the journey to Santiago. There were hidden messages not only on the board game but also along the physical way, on monuments or in churches or shrines. The game alerted pilgrims to dangers along the way and so the game was memorized and practiced so as not to be forgotten. Thus, the game became a kind of guide for the Camino.

I would be negligent if I failed to mention the town of Logroño on the Camino, where you can find the double-named square, *Plaza de Santiago* and *Plaza de la Oca* (*Saint James's Square* and *Goose Square*). Here appears a life-sized replica of the board game with images on flat square stones along with the gigantic die that serve as seats for visitors. Spain also had a TV program in the 1990's called Juego de Oca, but its resemblance to the medieval game is in name only. Even though it was set up like a board game, unlike the original board game, its goal was to win money through performing various stunts.

While the image of the goose and its symbolic footprint had much influence on the medieval pilgrimage to Santiago, the sign of the goose could not compete in replacing the scallop shell as the badge of recognition and honor. For that, I am thankful. I much prefer wearing the nice-looking scallop shell to a dried-up goose's appendage.

Chapter 5

Stories in Stone

Along the Camino you are bound to encounter stories displayed in architectural structures, such as pillars, domes, windows, walls, etc. One of the most amazing of these structures is the church called *San Pedro de la Rúa* (*Saint Peter's Street*) in the town of *Estella* (*Star*). Built in the twelfth and thirteenth centuries, it supposedly possesses a fragment of the True Cross along with Saint Andrew's shoulder bone. In the cloister are found Romanesque capitals on top of paired columns. The capital displays four scenes. Most of the scenes relate to a common story. The more intricate capitals display background visuals designed to connect the multiple scenes. Emotions and actions among the figures depicted are amazingly well captured in the stone. We see this in the reactions of some of the figures. Most of the stories portrayed are biblical, which is natural for a church setting. Others are allegorical and meant to portray Christian dogma or morals. Here are a few selections from these pillars.

On one pillar face we can see Christ visiting Limbo and freeing Adam and Eve, who are shown stepping on Satan.

Along with this we see demonic creatures carrying doomed souls in a basket. Another face of the capital shows Joseph of Arimatea and Nicodemus burying Christ. A third face of the capital displays Christ warning Mary Magdalene not to touch him. The fourth face of the capital shows the visit of the three Mary's to Christ's tomb.

There are also capitals depicting lives of the saints. One is of Saint Lawrence, another is of Saint Andrew and yet another is one of Saint Peter. On his capital he is standing before the ruler Herod Agrippa. The prison is to the right. The next face shows Peter taken to prison, followed by the third face showing him guarded by soldiers while an angel draws near and takes him by the hand. The final face is the city of Jerusalem.

Pilgrims will have the opportunity to see many churches and cathedrals along the Camino. They will undoubtedly be impressed with the massive display of stories found on their altars, walls and porticos. To list every one of these would entail a book in itself. So I will mention two of the most impressive cathedrals and some of their stories in stone: Burgos and Astorga.

The cathedral at Burgos is famous not only as a landmark for the city, but for all of Spain. Besides being declared a national heritage site, it is the burial site of Spain's national hero and his wife, Rodrigo Díaz de Vivar (better known as El Cid) and Doña Jimena. The title, El Cid, comes from Arabic and means, "Lord." In the epic poem, "El Cid," his title is *El Cid Campeador*, meaning *Lord Leader in the Field*. In popular English usage today the title has evolved to mean *Lord Champion*.

The cathedral also houses some very fine artwork. One

of the most common art forms of the Middle Ages is found in this magnificent cathedral: the stone-carved tombs of the nobles. Two of these tombs belong to the *condestable* (the man in charge after the king), Don Pedro Fernández de Velasco, and his wife, Doña Mencía de Mendoza. The story in these carved-marble effigies is simply one of trust and fidelity. While the sculptor has detailed everything from clothing to the veins on the hands, it is the small dog at the foot of the Doña that represents those desired qualities of trust and fidelity between a man and a woman. Furthermore, it was well known that the effigy of a dog on a medieval tombstone represented faithfulness by a wife in marriage.[1] The sleeping dog curled at his mistress's feet epitomizes and humanizes the trust and faithfulness. Dog lovers might feel compelled to reach out and pet this dog because of the emotional response it arouses. You expect it to rise at any moment and start wagging its tail or perhaps bark at approaching visitors.

There are also life-like sculptures in this cathedral. Some of them are so realistic as to be frightening. I almost thought the statue of Christ being scourged was a real person in pantomime. (You see a lot of pantomime in Spain, especially around tourist attractions.) I was backing away from a wall display and almost bumped into this statue. Luckily I turned just in time but the sight was overwhelming and I gasped out of the sheer fright believing this was a live person. When I realized it was a statue I was still awed at how realistic it looked.

As previously mentioned, the Cid is buried in this

---

1   Douglas Keister, *Stories in Stone: A Field Guide to Cemetery Symbolism and Iconography* (Salt Lake City, UT: Gibbs Smith, 2004), p. 72.

cathedral. However, there is a story pertaining to this. Originally the Cid's body was taken to the Monastery of San Pedro de Cardeña, a few klicks away from Burgos. It is the same place where he had left his wife and two daughters when he was forced into exile by the king. He had requested that he be buried with his horse, Babieca (the horse's name means "stupid," "idiot," or "foolish"). This horse was anything but stupid and I doubt if he were that the Cid would have survived as long as he did. Per the Cid's wishes, the horse was buried at the monastery; a tombstone marks the site. The body of the Cid ended up staying at the monastery for a few centuries. It was transferred to the Burgos Cathedral in 1921. Of course, there is a story or stories connected to this transfer and it is my pleasure to relate them to you.

For you aficionados of the Cid's life and for those of you who may have only seen the epic film of 1961, *El Cid*, you will recall that the dead Cid left Valencia strapped to his horse in an upright position with his raised sword in hand. His wife took him thusly to the monastery in Cardeña, where the body remained seated upright next to the main altar for the next ten years.

One of these legends was how his body was cared for during the ten years it remained seated at the side of the main altar. It is said Jimena begged the king to let her husband stay there as long as his body remained in good condition. According to records kept by the monks, the king consented:

…and sent for the high-backed chair which the Cid had brought him at Toledo. He ordered that the Cid should be seated on the right hand side of the altar, and that it should be covered by a rich golden brocade; and that behind the chair there a magnificent tabernacle to house the insignia of the Cid, together with those of Navarre and Aragón.[2]

Legend has it that they clothed his body in the richest garments, with his right hand holding his sword, *Tizón* or *Tizona* (its name means *burning stick*. The Cid also had another sword named *Colada* and means a sword made from metal without any impurities). They replaced his clothes when they started to look dirty or old. He stayed this way for ten years. Then his body started to fall apart. His nose fell off his face and the monks decided it was time to bury him. Even then he was not buried with his horse but entombed in the monastery's church along with his wife until the nineteenth century. During the ten years he sat in state at the side of the main altar, more legends began to spread about the Cid and his preserved condition in the monastery's church.

One such legend is sometimes referred to as "The Jew Who Thought to Tweak the Cid's Beard." Now, in those times it was considered a serious affront to have your beard tweaked or plucked. The Cid is remembered to have done such a thing to his enemy, Count García Ordóñez, and he did not just tweak it but tore some of it out. The Cid himself was so fearful that his own beard might be plucked that he wore protective netting on it. So with this in mind, our legend goes something like this.

One day during a festival at the monastery, a Jew steps inside the church. He stares at the seated Cid and when he sees

2   Stephen Clissold, *In Search of the Cid* (New York: Barnes & Noble, 1994), p.209.

there is no one around he reminds the Cid that no Christian or Moor had ever attempted to pull his beard. He says he is going to do so now and taunts the Cid in not being able to do anything about it. The Jew is stunned to see the Cid put his hand on his sword and withdraw the blade to a palm's length. The Jew faints from fright. When the festival goers come into the church and find him, they throw water on him to revive him. The Jew comes to and relates his story. As a result of his experience with the dead Cid, he converts to Christianity and takes the name, Diego Gil. He spends the rest of his life serving the monastery.

During the French invasion in the early nineteenth century some French soldiers vandalized the Cid's tomb and made off with some bones and his famous swords, *Tizona* and *Colada*. One of Napoleon's generals, General Thiebault, sought to right the vile actions of his countrymen. He ordered that what remained of the bones of the Cid and Jimena be collected and taken to Burgos where they could be properly buried and honored with a monument. In the interim, the general personally safeguarded the remains, which he wrapped in a shroud and placed under his bed. Thiebault wanted to make sure the Cid was a real person. He consulted two historians, one, an authoritative scholar, Llorente, was well known for his works on the Inquisition. Both consultants denied the existence of the Cid and concluded that he was a totally fictitious character. The general wisely ignored the decisions of the consultants and as a result the remains were put in the mausoleum that he had ordered built.

However, when the French were driven out of Spain, the monks petitioned that the remains of the Cid and his wife be restored to their original resting place. Their request was granted and in 1826, a funereal retinue marched the remains back to the monastery. Lo and behold the remains were moved again, nine years later. This was due to a government decree that took over the monastery and sold the land. The remains went to Burgos to rest in a chapel until 1921 when they were moved to their present location, the Cathedral of Burgos. The Cid was just as much in exile in death, if not more, as he was in life. As one scholar put it:

No hero, surely, unless it be the ever-roving Ulysses himself, has truly earned a better right to an undisturbed sleep than the Cid. Maybe Rodrigo and his Jimena now have found their final resting place at last,…[3]

In addition, Federico García Lorca, one of Spain's greatest twentieth-century poets, said, "In Spain, the dead are more alive than the dead of any other country in the world." These words seem to apply so appropriately to the numerous burial ceremonies of the Cid.

When his body was moved to the cathedral, church officials would not allow for the horse to be buried with him. He had to settle for his wife. This must have prompted a lot of jokes at the local *taberna* (*tavern*). I was a little disappointed that the Cid and his wife were not buried in carved marble tombs like the Condestable and his wife. Probably just as well since Babieca's effigy would be a bit large to place at the foot of the Cid. The actual burial site is in the center of the Cathedral. There is merely a roped-off section of red marble flooring with

---

3   Ibid., pp. 261–17.

a golden inscription that denotes their burial site. There seems to be plenty of space here in which the Cid's horse could have also found his resting place and fulfilled the wish of the Cid.

I began to feel a little sympathy for the Cid not having his faithful companion buried with him, until I saw the imposing painting hanging on one of the walls in the cathedral. The Cid is standing next to his beloved Babieca with his sword in hand and dressed in a belted white tunic. As a final comment on this painting, I certainly see why Charleton Heston in his younger years was chosen to play the role of the Cid in the movie. While they are not twins in appearance, they could certainly pass for kinsmen. Or maybe it is just good Hollywood make-up.

There are stories linked to Babieca and how the Cid chose Babieca for his horse. As legend has it, Rodrigo as a young boy visited his godfather, a monk, at his monastery. The monks raised horses for income and were quite famous for their breeds. The godfather had promised Rodrigo one of the horses when he reached the right age. Well, the time had come and Rodrigo told his godfather he wanted the white stallion that was grazing nearby in the field. His godfather admonished him for his choice, saying that the animal was *babieca* (*dumb, stupid,* or *idiot*). Rodrigo insisted and when he got the horse, he named him Babieca. The other version is that the godfather called Rodrigo *babieca*, meaning he was stupid for choosing such a horse. Yet another version has it that Rodrigo's father calls him *babieca* for choosing such a horse. Take your pick, the end results will still be the same. The horse went on to become one of the most famous war horses in history.

Many of the stories of the Cid are recorded in the

"Chronicle of the Cid". In the "Chronicle we read about the Cid's pilgrimage to Santiago and his famed encounter with a leper who turns out to be Saint Lazarus. The leper is caught in a quagmire and calls out for help. Most people would have feared this leper and found him to be quite repulsive because of the disfigurement rendered to the body by the disease. The Cid treats him with unusual and kind treatment. He shares his bed and food with him. Because the Cid shows such deep compassion for the leper, it is revealed to him in a dream that the leper is really Lazarus who promises the Cid that God will always help him.

What really connects the Cid to Santiago is the fact that he and Saint James have a common cause—the Reconquest. They become intertwined in the eyes of the people. They become symbols of Spain, one, a man of the people, and the other, a man of God. Not only do they have a common cause but they also have similar icons. Like Saint James, the Cid is depicted on a white horse with the heads of dead Moors at its feet. Thus, the Cid takes on the role of "Santiago the Moor Slayer". Moreover the stories of both men are mixed with elements of historical fact and legendary myth that energize the Spanish people on to victory. Even after the final victory, the expulsion of the Moors from Spain, these two heroes remain, Saint James, the patron saint of Spain, and El Cid, its national hero.

Moving on to Astorga, we encounter another cathedral embellished with stories in stone. The main entrance or portico is incredibly intricate leaving no free space of stone being untouched by some object or detail. It boggles the mind if not the eye to see so many complex details spaced so artistically. It is almost like watching scenes from coming attractions at the movies. You expect a continuance of the previous scene but the themes and subjects change rapidly as the eye moves from one tableau to the next. In the center of the portico is the display of Christ being taken down from the Cross. Numerous other tableaux radiate from this central scene. You see the expulsion of the money lenders from the temple by Christ. Then there is the story of the adulterous woman, where it seems she will be stoned by one of the men who appears to be picking up a stone. Another tableau depicts a man who is suffering from dropsy or edema. A blind man is cured by Christ's touch in yet another scene. It is noteworthy that the blind man is dressed like a pilgrim, that is, he has the traditional hat, staff, gourd and a scallop shell that adorns his staff. These are clearly items characteristic of the Santiago pilgrimage of the Middle Ages placed in a scene from the biblical era, making them just a little anachronistic or out of place in this timeframe.

In the interior of the cathedral on the main altar to the right of the center scene is the colorful sculpture telling the story of the wedding of Mary and Joseph. Mary appears to be pregnant and a bit hesitant. Her head is tilted downward and her expression does not seem to be a very happy one. In fact, the expressions of all the participants are very solemn, almost sad.

These stories in stone were crucial to Christians living during times when universal education was lacking and few had access to written works. Even if books were accessible, the everyday man probably did not know how to read. Many of the works were in Latin and this was also another hindrance. These stone works of art became great teaching tools for the Church. The stories in stone were visual and man could comprehend them, especially after hearing them repeatedly through sermons and religious presentations.

Biblical or religious stories abounded in the churches and cathedrals of medieval Spain, but they were not the only ones ingrained in stone. Secular literature also became immortalized in stone. The *Palacio de los Reyes de Navarra* (*Palace of the Navarre Monarchs*) in Estella has a capital that displays a passage from the epic poem, "Chanson de Roland," where Roland fights the giant, known as Ferracutus. The names of the combatants as well as the sculptor's name are inscribed in the stone. The actual battle is said to have taken place in Nájera, a town about thirty-five miles away from Estella and a major stop on the Camino. Before reaching the town of Nájera there is a stone hut in the shape of a medieval Frankish helmet that stands as a monument to Roland's battle with Ferracutus. You can enter the stone hut and even spend the night as evidenced by the debris left behind. There are stone benches on which to place a sleeping mat or one could lie on the floor for more room. The hut probably could hold four to six people and appears a safe shelter in inclement weather.

The helmet monument commemorates the legend in the PT or Book IV of the *Codex* where Roland does battle with the Saracen giant, Ferracutus, who holds the City of Nájera. In brief, they fight for two days, taking truces to rest at night. During the second night the sympathetic Roland places a stone beneath the head of the giant as a pillow, and upon waking the giant reveals to Roland that he is only vulnerable in one spot: his navel. In the next battle, Roland's dagger finds the spot and the giant is killed.

In another version of the legend the battle takes place at *Poyo de Roldán*, near the road to Alesón. The word *poyo* refers to the rock that Roland used in this version to kill Ferracutus, hence the location's name. This version aligns more with the biblical story of David and Goliath since both giants were killed with stones. While this legend has often been compared to the biblical story of David and Goliath, David's giant cannot compare in size to Roland's. Goliath is six and a half feet tall while Ferracutus is about twelve cubits, with a cubit being about eighteen inches. That would make him about eighteen feet tall. Like Goliath, he frightens off contenders before facing Roland. Roland wins not through military skill but through an almost sneaky maneuver. He places a stone pillow beneath the giant's head and when he awakens he reveals his physical weakness to Roland. The stone pillow that Roland places beneath the giant's head parallels the stone used by David to kill Goliath. The stone pillow becomes as much a death blow for Ferracutus as the slung stone does for Goliath.

In both stories, David and Roland are fighting for the "true religion." David tells Goliath that he comes against him "…in the name of the Lord of hosts, the God of the armies of Israel." (I Samuel, verse 45) In the *PT*, Roland and Ferracutus

…fall to disputing as to which holds the true religion. Roland undertakes to explain the doctrine of the Three-in-One, but the discussion reaches a stalemate and the pair resume their combat with the agreement that whichever wins shall be considered to have vindicated his own faith.[4]

---

4   Smyser, p. 33.

Again these stories are more fodder for the Church and Crown to spread propaganda for their causes, that is, to encourage men to follow the bravery and courage of an exemplar knight, join the crusade for the Reconquista and convert the disbelievers to Christianity.

Chapter 6

And The Word Was Made Spanish

Many pilgrims often took side trips to other shrines that were not too far from the Camino. The Monasteries of *San Millán de Cogolla* (*Saint Emilian's Cowl*) are situated about 21 km or about thirteen miles from the Camino after leaving Nájera and are popular with pilgrims today. The word "Cowl" refers to the cowl-like shape of the surrounding mountains and is most appropriate as it relates to the hooded cowl that the monks wore. There are two monasteries with the name of the saint plus the designating Latin words, *suso* or *yuso* (*suso* means *upper* and *yuso* means *lower*). San Millán Suso is the older, built in the sixth century while Yuso was built in the eleventh century. San Millán Suso lies higher up on a hill and San Millán Yuso is on a lower plain, hence the adjectives, suso and yuso.

In 1997, UNESCO declared the two monasteries a national heritage site because of the monastic practices from the sixth century to the present day. The monastery designated Suso became renowned as a scriptorium. Here the monks copied ancient texts, illuminating them with colorful artwork. The monks wrote marginal notes explaining the Latin, Greek, Arabic, or whatever language the text was in. The notes are called *glosas* in Spanish and *glosses* in English. These particular glosses came to be known as the *Glosas Emilianenses* (*Emilian Glosses*). The name is derived from the monastery itself and the glosses explain in Castilian or Spanish[1] what the foreign text means.

These glosses were originally thought to be the first appearance of written Spanish, but that has been disputed. The Spanish Royal Academy now says that documents found in the province of Burgos contain the first appearance of written Spanish. Even with this pronouncement, these glosses are noteworthy in many other aspects.

One aspect is that the monk who wrote these glosses was probably of Basque origin since he wrote at least two of them in Basque, a language spoken in northern Spain where this monastery is located. While the glosses are short, no more than six words, they are considered to be the first written words in Basque. There is a plaque that hangs in the monastery of San Millán Yuso displaying the glosses. So far, no one has disputed the Basque claim.

Another aspect of these glosses is that they are very numerous in this one manuscript. There are about a thousand of them. None of them is very long. Here is a copy of the

---

1   The term Castilian Spanish can be used in English for the specific dialects of Spanish spoken in north and central Spain. Sometimes it is more loosely used to denote the Spanish spoken in all of Spain as compared to Spanish spoken in Latin America. For the purpose of this book, I will refer to the language as Spanish to avoid any confusion.

longest one, which is a prayer. The text in the first column contains some rudiments of Spanish, Basque, and Aragonese.

Con o aiutorio de nuesto dueno Christo, dueno
salbatore, qual dueno get ena
honore et qual duenno tienet ela madatione con o patre con
o spiritu sanctu sancto en os sieculos de lo siecu
los Facamos Deus Omnipotes tal serbitio fere ke
denante ela sua face gaudioso segamus. Amen.[2]

With the help of our Lord Christ Lord
Savior, Lord who is in honor,
Lord that has command with the Father, with
the Holy Spirit forever and ever
God Omnipotent, make us do such a service that
before His face joyful we are. Amen.

Even if these glosses were not the first expressions to be written in Spanish, San Millán can still claim to be the birthplace of the first named poet to write in Spanish. Indeed, he wrote a near plethora of works during his lifetime. His name, Gonzalo de Berceo, (1197–1264) came from the village of Berceo, which is quite near to the monasteries where he spent most of his life. He is commonly called just Berceo when speaking of his works. His works consist mainly of religious themes and are the following:

"Los Milagros de Nuestra Señora"
"Los Loores de Nuestra Señora"
"El Duelo de la Virgen"
"La Vida de Santo Domingo de Silos"
"La Vida de San Millán de la Cogolla"

---

2   Wikipedia.org/wiki/Glosas_Emilianenses

"La Vida de Santa Oria"
"El Martirio de San Lorenzo"
"El Sacrificio de la Misa"
"Los Signos Que Aparecerán Antes Del Juicio Final"
"Los Himnos"

"The Miracles of Our Lady"
"The Praises of Our Lady"
"The Lamentation of the Virgin"
"The life of Saint Dominic of Silos"
"The life of Saint Emilio of Cogolla"
"The life of Saint Oria"
"The Martyrdom of Saint Lawrence"
"The Sacrifice of the Mass"
"The Signs Which Will Appear Before Judgment Day"
"The Hymns"

This may not seem like an overabundance of works, but take into account that these works were poems and some of them quite lengthy. The "Miracles of Our Lady" comprise 911 stanzas of four lines each, or 3,644 lines total. His "Life of Saint Dominic" runs 777 quatrains, or 3,108 lines. The poetic mode that Berceo employed for his works is called *mester de clerecia*, that is, a poetic mode used by the clergy, as opposed to the *mester de juglaría*, a poetic mode used by troubadours. The mode used by the clergy was in written form and very scholarly while the mode used by the troubadour was oral and lighter in subject matter. The *clerecia* mode is sometimes referred to as *cuaderna via* (*fourfold way*), because the quatrains are of four fourteen-syllable lines, each with a caesura or pause in the middle and a rhyming scheme of AAAA, BBBB, etc. Berceo's poems are the first written in Spanish in this metrical form. The monastery of San Millán de la Cogolla became known as the "cradle of the Spanish language" through these works.

Other versions of Berceo's poetic stories exist in various languages. For example, his Miracle 8 is a match to Miracle 17 in the Latin version of Book II in the *Codex*. It also matches Cantiga 26 in Alfonso El Sabio's (Alfonso The Wise) "Cantigas de Santa Maria" (*"Songs of Holy Mary"*). These poems are written in *Gallego-Portugués* (*Galician-Portuguese*), which was spoken in the northwest area of Spain during the medieval era. Bercero deliberately chose not to write in Latin but in *román paladino*, the term that refers to the common language of the people. Berceo even goes so far as to say his Latin is very poor, which we know is not true because most of his works are from Latin sources. While he does not translate verbatim he would need to know the content of his source in order to create the same story in another language. His modesty is for a good cause; he wants the people to be able to understand the poem just as if it were an everyday conversation with a neighbor. He says in "The Life of Saint Dominic": "I will compose a poem in the plain language used by the people for speaking to their neighbors, for I am not so learned as to create another text in Latin."[3]

In spite of his modesty for knowing Latin, he is not too modest in stating that his work might be "worth a glass of

---

3   Jeannie K. Bartha, Annette Grant Cash, and Richard Terry Mount, *The Collected Works of Gonzalo de Berceo in English Translation* (Tempe: Arizona Center for Medieval and Renaissance Studies, 2008), p. 223.

fine wine.">[4] He believed in his work and himself as a poet. In regards to Berceo's originality the medieval scholar, John E. Keller, points out:

…there is a special kind of originality in his works. He transposed the contents of his sources, the miracles of the Virgin and the lives of the saints (whatever their time or place), into the homely context of his familiar existence. He forged his nascent Castilian vernacular into a literary instrument, using it to create new and unusual vocabulary filled with words found nowhere else, yet perfectly understandable by all, including earthy expressions which are quite surprising.[5]

Now that we know a little about Berceo, that is, his importance to the development of the Spanish language and literature by way of his works and his connection to the Camino, we can look at one story that connects to the Camino. Number VIII, titled "The Pilgrim Deceived by the Devil," tells us of a "wanna be" monk. In brief, his name is Guiralt, and before entering the Cluny Monastery he decided to make a pilgrimage to Santiago to do penance for his sins, especially the sin of fornication. Before the pilgrimage he fornicates again instead of keeping the customary vigil. On his journey he unknowingly meets the Devil disguised as Saint James. The Devil tricks him into cutting off his penis in order to save his soul. The pilgrim does as the Devil orders, plus he slits his throat and dies excommunicated for his suicide. Saint James hurries to the place where a group of devils are carrying the pilgrim's soul off to hell. Saint James cries out, "Free," he said, "oh, evil ones, the prisoner that you carry, for he is not

---

4   Ibid.
5   Bartha et al., p. xvi.

quite as surely yours as you think;" (199)[6] Saint James earns his reputation as a "son of thunder," his sobriquet, by which he was known in biblical times, when he berates the Devil and says, "…you killed my pilgrim!" (202)[7] He continues to admonish the Devil's deceitful actions:

Had you not told him that you were Saint James, had you not shown him the sign of my scallop shells, he would not have harmed his body with his own scissors nor would he lie as he lies, outside in the road. I am greatly offended by your behavior; I consider my image mocked by you; you killed my pilgrim with a skillful lie. Moreover, I see his soul mistreated. (204)[8]

Saint James appeals to the Virgin Mary for judgment, that is who is right, the Devil or the pilgrim. Both the Devil and Saint James present their case before her. Mary rules in favor of the pilgrim because she says, "he thought he was obeying Saint James, and that in so doing he would be saved; the deceiver should suffer more."[9] Mary orders the soul to be returned to its body and the pilgrim to repent; then the pilgrim will be judged.

Berceo then tells us that all the pilgrim's wounds are healed. The scar from Guiralt's throat-cutting barely showed. His private parts that were cut off, however, never grew back. To ensure that the people understood

---

6   Gonzalo de Berceo, *Miracles of Our Lady*, Translated by Richard Terry Mount and Annette Grant Cash, (Lexington, KY: University of Kentucky Press, 1998), p. 51.

7   Ibid.

8   Berceo, pp. 51-2.

9   Ibid, p. 52

his condition, Berceo adds that Guiralt was capable of urinating because a hole remained in place of his private part. Guiralt finishes his pilgrimage, goes back home and enters the monastery as a penitent. We are told that he lived a good life as a monk until his death.

Berceo includes some lines to suggest that this poem and others like it were recited for the pilgrims when he writes, "Such a thing as this we must write down, those who are yet to come will take pleasure in hearing it."[10] Thus, Berceo preserves the lore of the Camino. A toast to Berceo!

---

10   Ibid, p. 53.

The ossuary at Roncesvalles and its macabre remains.

The Town Hall (Ayuntamiento) in Pamplona

Metal sculpture (1996) by Navarre artist, Vicente Galbete, at Alto del Perdón. It simbolizes the history of the pilgrimage from its beginning to present day.

Monument to a cyclist who died on the Camino

A typical rollo jurisdiccional in Boadilla. It is a symbol of the town's judicial power.

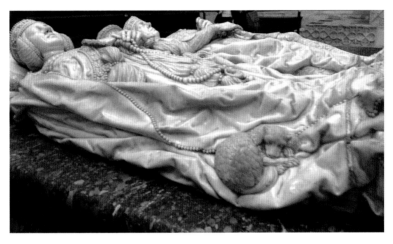

Tombs of El Condestable, Pedro Fernández de Velasco, and his wife, Doña Mencía Mendoza, in the Burgos Cathedral

El Cid and his horse, Babieca, in the Burgos Cathedral

The knight, Suero de Quiñones defended his honor at the Órbigo bridge. It is one of the longest Romanesque bridges in Spain.

Mary and Joseph's marriage, depicted at the main altar tableau in the Astorga Cathedral

Helmet-shaped monument to Roland, author in foreground

Chickens in Cathedral de Santo Domingo in commemoration of the most famous legend of the Camino.

Monte de Gozo Monument with Pope John Paul II depicted in sculpture embracing Saint James in the traditional pilgrim way (That's me in foreground.)

The church of Nuestra Señora de la Barca before fire of December 2013

Chapter 7

Construction Workers
And "Fowl Play"

Part I: Construction Workers

After leaving the monasteries of San Millán and rejoining the Camino, our next jaunt down the road brings us to *Santo Domingo de la Calzada* (*Saint Dominic of the Road*), a town of just a little over six thousand people; and beyond that about twenty-five miles is the tiny berg of *San Juan de Ortega* (*Saint John's Nettle*), population thirty. Saint Dominic was Saint John's mentor and apprenticed him to aid pilgrims by showing him how to build roads, bridges, hospitals and refuges. In addition, the lives of these two saints are linked in various other ways.

Both saints had monikers or nicknames and lived in the wild. Saint John took the name *Ortega* from the location known as Urteca or Ortega where he erected a hermitage for himself. Saint Dominic's nickname, of course, is associated with his life's work, which is, building or improving roads for pilgrims. Saint John was more of an intellectual than Saint Dominic in that he finished his studies in a monastery and founded a monastery; meanwhile, Saint Dominic was asked to leave the monastery due to his poor scholastic performance. Too bad the monasteries did not have industrial art classes, better known as "shop classes," because Dominic would have been a top student with his skills of road and bridge building.

Both saints have tombs where pilgrims and tourist can pay their respects. Saint Dominic's tomb resides in the cathedral named for him, and Saint John's resides in the church named for him. From their names come the names for the towns in which they are buried. Both lived in the eleventh and part of the twelfth centuries, Saint Dominic (1019–1109) and Saint John (1080–1163). Both dedicated their lives to helping the pilgrim. Incidentally, both had legends or stories associated with them that continue to be retold through the ages.

One of the legends associated with Saint Dominic has two versions. In one version the townsfolk give permission to Dominic to cut down as many trees as he can in a day's time. When he paused to pray, angels continued to chop the trees for him. In another version of this legend, he made only one cut and the tree fell. However, by sunset he had all the wood he needed.

Saint John came to be known as the patron saint of hospice keepers, children and barren wives. The reason for this according to one author is, when "…his tomb was opened, there was a pleasant odor, and out flew a swarm of white bees, which were interpreted to be the souls of unborn children that the saint was keeping safe pending their incarnation in the wombs of the faithful."[1] As a result of this patronage, women

---

1   Gitlitz et al., p. 168.

came to his shrine and/or prayed to him for a child. One of the most famous women to visit his shrine and pray for a child was Queen Isabel, the Catholic Monarch. She named her first child Juan. She returned to the shrine to pray for another child and soon had a daughter whom she named Juana. Unfortunately, her son died at the age of nineteen, either of tuberculosis or, according to court rumor, over-indulging in sexual activity. (Couldn't doctors differentiate between the two in that era? Whoa, here's a research project waiting to happen and I bet it could get government funds to do it.) To add to Isabel's woes, her daughter went mad and had to be locked up after her husband died. Juana insisted that her husband's dead body accompany her everywhere because she believed a miracle would happen and he would return to life.

Over a hundred miracles are attributed to San Juan de Ortega. Three of them relate directly to pilgrims. The first states that some pilgrims were praying near the grave of their child and laid some apples on the tomb. It is recorded that the child called out for one of the apples and was restored to life. The second miracle involved a French pilgrim, Vadovin, who was terribly crippled and so deformed that he had to be fed by others. He gets cured. Another miracle involving a pilgrim was a man on crutches who swore he would not leave the shrine until he was cured. His fellow pilgrims said they could hear his muscles and nerves being stretched while he was being cured.

Of the two saints' shrines, Saint Dominic's is by far the most popular site for pilgrims and tourists. It is not necessarily the saint's reputation and tomb that attracts them, but of all things, a chicken coop and a legend that has endured through the centuries of pilgrimages to Santiago. It has become the most popular legend on the Camino which you will discover in Part II of this chapter.

Part II: When a Rooster Crows and a Hen Cackles, or Chickens Rule

The chicken coop resides in the cathedral of Santo Domingo de la Calzada near the south door on an elevated niche. It has an ornamental grille covering a glass panel on the front of it. The fowl can be seen walking around inside the glass enclosure. It is well lit, but difficult to photograph because the bright lighting causes too much reflection or glare and blends in with the whiteness of the chickens. There are sculpted likenesses of both the rooster and the hen on separate panels on either side of the enclosure.

The legend of the miracle of the hanged pilgrim was spread in the early 1100s. Again, there exist several versions of the story. A few to mention are those of Berceo, Alfonso The Wise and the author(s) of the *Codex*, Book II. Not all versions include the chickens but all include the main plot of a pilgrim who is accused by the innkeeper or innkeeper's daughter of stealing a goblet and is consequently hung. As to the popularity of the story, I quote a footnote marked number 553 in the work, *The Miracles of Saint James*, by Coffey, et al.: "This is probably the most popular of the St. James's miracles throughout time. Versions have been created in prose, poetry, sculpture and painting through the nineteenth century, in England, France, Germany, Portugal and Switzerland."[2]

---

2   Coffey, et al., p. 139.

Indeed the list of examples for finding this legend in various genres worldwide attests to its dispersion and popularity. The art museum in Indianapolis, Indiana, has a fifteenth-century retablo that narrates the story in multiple panels. The external walls of a private chapel in Tafers, Switzerland, display the story. In English literature, Robert Southey wrote, "The Pilgrim to Compostela," which recounts the legend.

The version of this legend perpetuated by the town and cathedral of Santo Domingo de la Calzada, tells that the family is German and the son's name is Hugonell. In other versions, the family is French and no name is given for the family or son. At the evening meal the innkeeper's daughter takes a fancy to the young man and makes coquettish advances toward him. The young man does not respond to her flirtations and she feels scorned. For revenge she hides a silver goblet in the young man's knapsack.

The next morning the young man and his parents have barely set out again on their journey to Santiago when they see and hear a group of the townspeople yelling at them to stop. When they do, they are searched as suspects for stealing the goblet. When they find it in the knapsack of the young man, they arrest him and take him to the local magistrate. He is declared guilty in spite of his crying pleas of innocence. He is immediately hung, to the horror of his parents. In this version, the parents make one last visit to the square where their son is hanging before leaving for Santiago. They see that their son is still alive and go running to the magistrate's house to tell him that their son is alive. The magistrate, who has just sat down to a meal of roasted chickens, was very annoyed by their intrusion and refused to be bothered. When the parents persist, the magistrate exclaims that their son is no more alive than the roasted chickens on his dining table. At that very moment, the chickens rise from the platter and begin to crow and cackle, complete with feathers. The magistrate is somewhat humbled and releases the son. In some versions, the girl responsible for the treacherous act is burned alive or sent to a convent for the rest of her life to do penance.

In another version of the story, the parents continue on to Santiago and on their return they stop to visit their son's grave. They are surprised and startled to see that their son is still hanging from the scaffold and even more surprised and startled to see that he is still alive. (Didn't anybody else in the town notice this?) The son explains to them that (a) the Virgin Mary, (b) Saint James, (c) Saint Dominic, or (d) all of the preceding saved him (take your pick, since the various versions of this story have different people responsible for saving the young man. I put the last choice "d" to cover all bases.) The one responsible for saving him did so by placing her/his/their hands beneath his feet to support him.

As mentioned previously, some versions of the legend do not have any chickens in them. The chickens do not appear in the versions by Berceo, Alfonso The Wise, or the version that is in the *Codex*. The common link among these stories is that a person is hung for stealing a globlet and remains alive for several days while some saint or the Virgin Mary holds him up by placing their hands beneath the person's feet. With that noted, this "chicken" story is still the most popular legend on the Camino.

So where did the version with the chickens originate?

The version with the chickens as participants appears to be a late version, that is, it was written after Berceo, Alfonso and the *Codex* versions. The miracle of the resurrected cock and hen seems to be a fifteenth-century addition to the tale. Maria Jesús Lacarra states in her study that the earliest mention of the chickens with this legend is 1417 and that Juame Roig, a well-known Valencian writer of that era, also wrote a version of the legend including the chickens around 1460.[3] However, a version that includes the chickens could have been known by the mid fourteenth century since there are documents from Pope Clemente VI dated 1350 asking for and receiving permission to allow these live animals to live inside the church as a reminder of the miracle that took place there. Although the original stone coop dates from the latter half of the fifteenth century, they could have had a different coop or changeable location in the church until the permanent coop was built. There is mention that at one time they were boxed near the altar.

As mentioned earlier, Robert Southey, the English poet, wrote a version of this legend in the early nineteenth century. In his version the villainous innkeeper's daughter is punished by being sent to a nunnery to spend the rest of her life doing penance as a nun. The pilgrims are French and not German, as they are in some of the other versions. What is unique about Southey's version is his focus on the chickens and the humor he imparts though them in the poem. The poem has

---

3   María Jesús Lacalla, *Cuentos Y Leyendas en el Camino De Santiago* (*Stories and Legends on the Way of St. James*) (Zaragosa: Intitución Fernando El Católico, 2005), pp. 297–8.

an almost juvenile-like verse that is reminiscent of a Mother
Goose nursery rhyme. The following lines attest to this as the
chickens spring to life:

So up rose the Fowls in the dish,…
The Cock would have crowed if he could;
To cackle, the hen had a wish;
And they both slipped about in the gravy,
Before they got out of the dish.
And when each would have opened his eyes,
For the purpose of looking about them,
They saw they had no eyes to open,
And that there was no seeing without them.
All this was to them a great wonder;
They staggered and reeled on the table;
And either to guess where they were,
Or what was their plight, or how they came there,
Alas! They were wholly unable.
Because, you must know, that that morning-
A thing they had thought very hard
The cook had cut off their heads,
And thrown them away in the yard.
The Hen would have pranked up her feathers,
But plucking had sadly deformed her;
And for want of them she would have shivered with cold,
If the roasting she had had not warmed her.
And the Cock felt exceedingly queer;
He thought it a very odd thing
That his head and his voice were he did not know where,
And his gizzard tucked under his wing.
The gizzard got into its place.
But how, Santiago knows best;
And so, by the help of the Saint,
Did the liver and all the rest.
The heads saw   their way to the bodies;
In they came from the yard, without check;

And each took its own proper station,
To the very great joy of the neck.
And in flew the feathers, like snow in a shower,
For they all became white on the way;
And the Cock and the Hen in a trice we fledged,
And then who so happy as they?
"Cluck! Cluck!" cried the Hen right merrily then;
The Cock his clarion blew;
Full glad was he to hear again
His own Cock-adoo-del-doo![4]

In addition, Southey informs us how the chickens produce heirs with laying only two eggs and each following generation does the same. The original two chickens are shown to lead exemplary lives as a loving couple and when they die, they are buried side by side. From this version we learn too how the cock and hen became part of the city's coat of arms:

And, lest the fact should be forgotten,
(Which would have been a pity,)
'Twas decreed, in honour of their worth,
That a Cock and Hen should be borne thenceforth
In the arms of that ancient City.[5]

Some trivia linked to the story: the town of Santo Domingo de la Calzada has the following motto: *Donde la gallina cantó después de asar* (*Where the hen sang* or *cackled after roasting*). When visiting the cathedral it is considered good luck to find a chicken feather or to hear them crowing and cackling. The chickens that currently live in the coop are

---

4   Robert Southey, "The Pilgrim to Santiago" (Internet: www.pricejb. pwp.blueyonder.co.uk/ transcribed by John Price, 2006), pp. 10–11.

5   Ibid., p. 15.

considered heirs of the resuscitated roasters.

The town of Santo Domingo de la Calzada is a paradise for shoppers of chicken-shaped paraphernalia. If you are a fan of chickens or have friends that are, here is the place to find and buy such items. In addition, there are chickens shaped in candies, cakes and pastries. Pins, ceramics and things you never dreamed of are in the shape of a chicken in this town. You name it and you will probably find the chicken-shaped item there. Unfortunately, I don't have any friends who are chicken lovers except for the kind that are southern fried or roasted.

A cathedral with live chickens bothers me slightly. After all, the Cid wanted to be buried with his horse and the Church would not allow it. Yet, the Church allows live chickens to have an elaborate habitat in a cathedral because of a legend. The Cid was a real person and he was originally buried at a monastery with his horse close by. These are not legends, but facts. Seeing live chickens running around inside a remote village church is not uncommon but chickens cooped in a lavish cathedral in a display case is not the norm and appears so bizarre, which is probably the real reason many people visit the cathedral. They just do not believe it until they see it. Then again, it probably was not a bad move on the Church's part, since it certainly has been a way to attract people and stimulate the economy. It seems ironic, though, that the Cid, the national hero of Spain, cannot have his faithful steed, that fought as bravely as he did, lie alongside of him in death as he did in life. So chickens rule!

Chapter 8

Camino Miracles

The distance from Santo Domingo de la Calzada to Carrión de los Condes is just a little over ninety-five miles (160 km). Traveling through this stretch of the Camino will lead you to many churches and monuments where you may learn of the legends attached to them. Many are unique and not mentioned in any guidebook. Here are a few that I encountered.

About half way between Santo Domingo de la Calzada and the town of Grañón you encounter an imposing iron cross which stands near the left side of the trail. It is named *La cruz de los valientes* (*Cross of the Brave*) and is so named because of a famous conflict that was resolved here. It commemorates an event which took place here in the fourteenth century and the story goes something like this:

There was a dispute over some land that lay between the two towns of Santo Domingo and Grañón. The dispute escalated to the brink of an all-out war between the two towns. Fortunately, the town leaders had the good sense to reach a resolution that was agreeable to both sides. The fate of the land in question was to be decided through individual combat. That is, each town would provide one individual who would fight each other. The winner would claim the land for his town. The town of Grañón selected a common laborer, named Martín García. We do not know the name of the man selected by the town of Santo Domingo. What we do know is that the people of Santo Domingo were a bit deceitful in their preparation of the fight. They fed their man quite well and on the very day of the fight they greased his body with oil so Martín would have a hard time grabbing and holding his opponent. In the end, it did not matter; Martín overcame the odds to win the day. To this very day, the people of Grañón honor their hero and make a short pilgrimage every year on August 20th to this cross which marks the location of the combat. It is too bad countries today can't settle their differences this way.

Between Belorado and San Juan de Ortega is the tiny village of Villafranca Montes de Oca. Miracle 3, as told in the *Codex*, is said to have occurred here. As the story goes, a certain Frenchman desiring children married but was having no luck in impregnating his wife. He thought his lack of an heir was due to his innumerable sins. So he and his wife decided to make a pilgrimage to Santiago. Once at the shrine he pleaded and begged Saint James to help him. His request was granted and he soon had a son.

After the boy turned fifteen, the couple decided to return to Santiago to give thanks. They got as far as Villafranca Montes de Oca and the lad became very ill and died. The parents suffered with grief, and the mother implored Saint James to give her back her son else she would commit suicide. Saint James conceded to her request and resurrected the boy. The boy then relates how wonderful it had been to be with Saint James in the afterlife as compared to the misery of the present one, which displays the *contemptus mundi* theme that was characteristic of the Church's teachings during the medieval era. The son bemoans the fact that he has to return to an earthly life but at the same time is grateful to the saint. The family continues on to Santiago to give thanks. The rest of this miracle tale is spent on explaining how a dead man (Saint James) can bring another dead man (the son) back to life. The reason given is that Saint James is not really dead, but alive and living with God. He also is a saint and can, therefore, do such things.

Another twelve kilometers and we are at the town of San Juan de Ortega. The monastery in this town has a logbook of recorded miracles. The records date from 1756 and "… log 114 miracles granted to petitioners who had sought the intercession of San Juan de Ortega or San Nicolás de Bari here."[1] One of the miracles involved the Frenchman, Vadovin, whom we met in an earlier chapter in connection with our initial encounter with San Juan de Ortega. Vadovin's miraculous cure can be seen in the monastery's logbook.

About twenty-five miles from Burgos is the pilgrimage town of Castrogeriz. In the town is the church called *Santa María Del Manzano* (*Holy Mary of the Apple Tree*). It used to be a collegiate church (a church where the daily office of worship is maintained by a college of canons; a non-monastic, or a secular community of clergy) but is considered an ex-

---

1   Gitlitz et al., p. 168

collegiate church currently. As legend has it, this church owes a lot to Santiago and the Virgin Mary for its origin. It is believed by the faithful that Santiago had a vision as he was passing by this area. He saw the Virgin in an apple tree and got so excited that he jumped on his horse too hard, causing the horse's hoof prints to become embedded in a rock. The hoof prints can still be seen in the rock today near the south door of the church.

Four of the poems in Alfonso El Sabio's *Cantigas de Santa María* represent miracles linked with the construction of this church. These are stories written during the thirteenth century in poetic form and the Gallego-Portugués dialect. There are four hundred and twenty-seven of these compositions; not all were composed by Alfonso but he is considered to be the director or mentor for most and the author of many. These compositions were meant to be sung and each has musical accompaniment composed by the troubadours of the thirteenth century. Moreover, what make these compositions so unique are the exquisite illuminated miniatures that are found with them in the manuscripts. The artwork is not only a reflection of life in this period but it also portrays the story via another form. For these artistic miniatures tell the same story that the words reveal. Many of them are adapted from earlier pagan legends, but this is in keeping with the Church's command to alter and adapt pagan lore to Christian belief just as they had done with pagan festivals and statues. Even though the Cantiga repeats legends that other authors have treated, they are unique not just because of their multitude, but moreover because they are expressed through three different media: written word, music and illustrations. Each

Cantiga was set to music by court troubadours and explicit illuminated miniatures repeat the story in a picture format. What is astounding is that each poem's song has its own melody that fits the mood of the story. That is, if the story has a light tone, the music matches and vice versa. There are three times more the number of illuminated miniatures than there are Cantigas to illustrate and bring these stories to life. A good source on the study of these miniatures is John E Keller and Richard P Kinkade's Iconography in Medieval Spanish Literature. For purposes of summarizing these stories, I used an English translation written in prose and all summaries of the Cantigas are from Kathleen Kulp-Hill's work.[2]

In Cantiga 242, a stonemason slips and starts to fall from a wall he is working on. He calls out to the Virgin to save him and because he has been so faithful to her, Mary grabs him by the fingernails and holds him suspended for a greater part of the day. Help finally comes and they lay the worker before Mary's altar, where he then weeps with joy. He makes the miracle known throughout the land.

Another worker in Cantiga 249 falls from the very top of the church. As he is falling he cries out to the Virgin and she saves him, even after his head hits the rocks below. His saving, as we are told, is due to his devotion to Mary and his refusal of payment for his work. He was doing it out of love for Mary.

Cantiga 252 relates how Mary saved some workmen from being buried alive in sand when the ground collapsed. Many of the workers appeared to be killed; however, the rescuers

---

2   Kathleen Kulp-Hill, *Songs of Holy Mary of Alfonso X, the Wise* (Tempe: Arizona Center for Medieval and Renaissance Studies, 2000).

found them alive when they finally dug them out of the sand. The workmen had prayed to the Virgin and thus they were revived and kept safe until the rescue.

All four of the Cantigas mention the town of Castrogeriz and the Church of Holy Mary of the Apple Tree, including Cantiga 266. In 266, a large number of people are in the church to hear a sermon. A large beam begins to break away from the ceiling and fall on this crowd, but the Virgin intervenes and nobody gets hurt.

Alfonso succeeds in his purpose for writing these Cantigas. He wishes to praise and glorify Mary. He uses phrases such as "This is in praise of Holy Mary..." to begin his song starting with Cantiga 1 and the start of each decade (that is, with numbers 10, 20, 30, 40, etc., up to and including number 409). Alfonso was pretty straightforward in this purpose since he states it directly in his prologue when he writes, "And that which I seek is to praise the Virgin, Mother of Our Lord, Holy Mary the most wondrous of His creations."[3] However, this is not his only purpose; he also uses his poems to teach and spread Christian beliefs. In addition, he has a political motive. He has contributed much to the particular church he cites and he wants it to become known so that it will draw an audience who will contribute to it monetarily. The more the church is famed, the more people will come, and in turn more monetary deposits will be left at the church.

Now you can begin to understand how Alfonso got the title, "the Wise." In all fairness, he was quite an intellectual,

---

3   Kulp-Hill Kathleen, p. 2.

with his center of learning and school of translators. He was one of the greatest producers of written works during the late thirteenth century. In addition to translations of classical works, he produced a history of the world and a code of laws that is the basis for Spanish law. Moreover, his portrait in marble relief along with twenty-two other notables, hangs over the gallery doors of the House Chamber in the US Capitol Building. He and the others are noted for their work in establishing the principles that underlie American law.

As an aside and as legend has it, Alfonso is also responsible for creating that lovely tradition the Spaniards have in the late afternoon or early evening, that is, indulging in those wonderful aperitifs called *tapas* or *pintxos* in Basque. They are also a big hit with pilgrims on the Camino. According to the lore, Alfonso became concerned that there were too many tavern brawls caused by men who became quickly intoxicated because of empty stomachs. So he ordered tavern owners to supply patrons with tasty bits of food along with the wine in order to slow down intoxication and avoid drunken brawls. Of course this is legend and another version has the king prescribing these dishes because he was once stricken with a serious illness which only allowed him to take in small portions of food with small amounts of wine. After recovering from his illness, the king declared that no wine should be served at drinking establishments unless it was served with food. A variation on the legend proposes that the order was actually given to prevent peasants, who could often not afford both wine and food, to drink on an empty stomach since they would tend to choose drink over buying something nourishing to eat. Other historians believe tapas may have originated with farmers who consumed small meals accompanied by wine throughout the workday. Now Alfonso did not assign the name "tapas" to these tasty tidbits or snacks, which by the way means "cover" or "lid" in English. No, that honor goes to King Alfonso XIII of the twentieth century. His story goes as follows.

Sometime in the early twentieth century, King Alfonso XIII was either on a hunting trip or paying an official visit to Andalucía or maybe both when he stopped at a tavern to refresh himself. He asked for a glass of wine and when the waiter served it, the glass was covered with a piece of cheese or ham depending on the legend you read. The waiter explained that he had covered the glass to prevent any sand from getting into the glass due to the strong winds blowing that day. When the king ordered a second glass of wine, he asked that it be served with the same "cover" or "tapa." And as they say, the rest is history

About sixteen miles down the road from Castrogeriz, is the town of Frómista. Here resides the *Iglesia de Santa María del Castillo* (*Church of Holy Mary of the Castle*). It is said that a man excommunicated for not repaying money lent to him by Jews was unable to receive the Eucharistic Host. When he repented and was reinstated, the Host entered his mouth without any assistance. Centuries thereafter the church used a reliquary to exhibit the gold paten and "reluctant Host" to visiting pilgrims.

Other legends and miracles in Frómista are tied to San Martín (Saint Martin) and the exquisite church of the same name. This church, constructed in 1066, is considered one of the finest examples of Romanesque architecture in Spain. Here it is said San Martín preached fiery sermons, one of which concerned the decorum of unmarried women. According to the story, many unmarried women wore revealing necklines and fashions that were seen as immodest. One day one of these women dressed immodestly entered the church to attend mass. To make matters worse she began to flirt with the young men in the church, winking and laughing at them. San Martín became enraged and yelled thunderously at the woman to keep on laughing because she was soon to meet her doom. At that very moment, she collapsed before the frighten attendees and two unrecognized men entered the church. Their dress and hair style were that of Muslims and they carried the woman away never to be heard of again. The church and its attendees were so overcome with the strong smell of sulfur that the censer had to be used to restore some decent air to the church. It was only after a long period of time that the stench finally dissipated. From that time on, young women began to wear a hood to guard their modesty. The story also became a didactic lesson for young girls as it was repeated to them by their mothers when instructing them on how to dress. They warned them not to deviate from modest fashion or else they might end up like the woman in the story.

Another legend that concerns San Martín is one where the devil impersonates him and deceives dying men so that they change their wills. One such man was on the verge of retracting a donation that he had made to a hospital because of being duped by this impersonator. The man is in a trance-like state and knows something is not right. He calls upon San Martín for help. At that moment, San Martín pushes open the door of the man's room with a strong strike of his crosier and asks the man what is the matter. The man tells San Martín that here is another man who calls himself San Martín. This causes the real San Martín to strike the faker on the nape of the neck with his crosier and tell him to leave. What is significant is that he calls the faker by his name, Satan, and tells him to return to the place he came from, that is, hell.

While in Frómista should you happen to come upon a statue of San Telmo, also known as Saint Elmo or Blessed Peter González Telmo, do not confuse this saint with the Italian Saint Elmo. The diminutive *Elmo* (*Telmo*) belongs to the martyr-bishop, Saint Erasmus (died c. 303), an Italian saint who is the patron saint of sailors and associated with Saint Elmo's fire. Our Spanish Telmo never really became a saint. He only reached the blessed or beatification stage. However, he is considered the patron of Spanish and Portuguese sailors.

Walking another nine miles (15 km) from Frómista, you arrive in the town of Villalcázar de Sirga. Here you will find the church of *Santa María la Blanca* (*Holy Mary the White Virgin*).

The White Virgin, whose statue resides in this church, is said to have inspired many of Alfonso's Cantigas. Again, because many miracles were attributed to her at this church, Alfonso had a great opportunity and motive to spread her fame through his poetic songs, which attracted the pilgrims to this church and thus kept it well maintained with their contributions.

There are over a dozen Cantigas that take place in this church or make mention of the church. In Cantiga 31, a farmer who lives in Segovia has lost his dearly beloved pregnant cow. He fears it will be eaten by wolves or badly bitten, as has happened to other cows in the vicinity. He begs Mary to find his cow and if she does, he will give her the calf. The cow comes home and soon gives birth to a healthy calf. However, the farmer does not keep his promise but tries to sell the calf at the market. On the way to market, the calf runs away and the farmer is unable to catch or find it. The calf, according to the poet, showed itself to be very wise since it went directly into the church of Santa María la Blanca. There it stayed and it became a hardworking ox. It never had to be goaded or beaten to produce work and it became known as the best working animal of all the beasts that could pull or endure hard labor. Eventually the farmer found the animal and was described as being dumbfounded. He sent out an announcement concerning this animal and people came to hear him tell what happened to his calf and him.

In Cantiga 217, a French count tried to enter the church, but because he had not confessed his sins, he was unable to enter. Even with a band of ten knights who tried to push him through the entrance, he was still not able to enter. They pushed him so hard that blood ran from his mouth and nostrils. When this happened, the count began to repent and made his confession. Then he was able to enter the church effortlessly and in so doing began to praise the Virgin. Everyone there gave praise to the Virgin and spread the word about the miracle.

Cantiga 218 concerns a crippled German. This man was paralyzed on both sides and in the hands and feet. While he was very wealthy, his condition was costly and he soon became poor. He saw that a group of pilgrims were setting out to Santiago, so he asked if they would take him along with them. Hesitant about his request because of his poor condition and his poverty, they finally relented and agreed to take him along. They carried him with great difficulty and finally made it to Santiago. Unfortunately he was not cured there because of his sins. On the way home the pilgrims discovered that he had become blind. They decided it would be best to leave him at the church of Santa María la Blanca. There he called out to the Virgin, who in turn, cured him. He returned to his home and with the generous gifts given him, gave them as offerings to the Virgin.

In retrospect to these miracles, it seems that the Virgin outdoes Saint James because she is responsible for most of the cures in this area of the Camino. This is confirmed in a few other miracles, too. It is almost like the two are in competition and perhaps they were in those days. Bishops and kings wanted their shrines to be financially gainful so they could be maintained. Thus the more miracles attributed to a shrine the greater the possibility for income. I wonder, could this be the reason for the appearance of so many versions of the same story? The plots are the same. The big difference seems to be the hero or heroine.

Turning to Cantiga 227 we find a squire whom the Virgin rescues from a Moorish prison without anyone seeing him escape. While he is in prison he begins to cry miserably and the Moorish guard inquires why he cries so. He replies that back in his town they are celebrating the great feast of the Virgin and he is missing it. With that the guard orders him to be beaten mercilessly and thrown into the dungeon. While in the dungeon he prays to the Virgin and asks to be rescued because he is only in the dungeon because of talking about her to the Moor. She rescues him because of his praise for her and because he has gone faithfully every year to the Church of Santa María la Blanca to observe the feast of her assumption into heaven. She breaks his chains and irons and he slips by the Moors, who do not see him because they are at prayer. When he gets home he goes directly to the church with the iron that he had on his leg and tells everyone how the Virgin saved him.

Cantiga 229 tells how the Virgin blinds and paralyzes the Moors for trying to destroy her church, Santa María la Blanca. The Moors tried to tear the church down and they tried to burn it. No matter what they tried, not a stone was loosened. Instead, the Virgin made them lose strength in their limbs and struck them blind so that they had to be carried out of the church.

Cantiga 232 relates how a knight loses his hunting bird, a hawk, while out hunting. This hawk was a great hunter. He would catch heron, ducks and many other kinds of prey. His speed and grace were legendary. So when the knight could not find his bird after four months of searching, he had a waxen image of it made. He took the image to the church of the Virgen la Blanca and called upon her to find the bird. When he got back home, the bird was sitting on its perch. The knight gave a prayer of thanks while taking his hawk gently in his hand. This Cantiga has been recorded with music on a CD along with several other Cantigas. Produced by Nimbus Records and played by The Martin Bess Ensemble, the disc is titled *Cantigas de Santa Maria of Alfonso X*. There are twenty-two Cantigas in total. Number thirteen sings the story of this knight and his hawk. They are a fine example of the legends set to music.

Mary cures a deaf-mute boy in Cantiga 234. It occurs because of a nobleman who was in charge of raising the boy, took him to the very same church, Santa María la Blanca. There he laid him before the altar to sleep the night. The nobleman had the mass said and during the mass, the boy's tongue began to loosen and his ears opened. By the time mass finished, the boy could speak and hear very well.

How Mary saved some falconers from drowning is the subject of Cantiga 243. These were not just any falconers, but falconers of King Alfonso X, as stated in the poem. Their falcons drove some ducks into the river and in panic the ducks sank under the ice on the river. The falconers tried to retrieve the ducks but fell through the ice and were trapped. They prayed to the Virgin and were saved. They immediately go to the church of Santa María la Blanca to praise and give thanks. They also told the story to the king and his knights and, of course, the king composed a poem about it.

Cantiga 253 is another example of the Virgin superseding Saint James. Here a man receives as his penance the command to make a pilgrimage to Santiago from his home in Toulouse. Not only does he have to do the pilgrimage in order to be forgiven, he has to carry an iron staff that weighs twenty-four pounds to put at Saint James's altar. On the way he stops in the church of Santa María la Blanca and begs forgiveness. Wonders of wonders, the staff splits in two pieces. No one is able to lift either piece, and the man is released from his penance. He did continue to Santiago, telling everyone along the way of his miracle.

Cantiga 268 depicts a paralyzed woman who has many

candles lit at the church of Santa María la Blanca. She, too, is cured and becomes the lifelong servant of the Virgin.

Cantiga 278 is a bundle of miracles and at the same time proof of the propaganda spread to entice pilgrims to come to the shrine of La Blanca. A blind woman is cured on her way home from Santiago. Score another one for the Virgin. The cured woman meets a blind man on his way to Santiago and tells him about her cure. She advises him to go to the Virgin's shrine. He goes to the Virgin's shrine and is also cured. We are not told if he went to Santiago or not. Score still another one for the Virgin. There is almost blatant evidence in this poem that popularizing a shrine brings monetary gain. "She (the Virgin) cured many people of ailments and revived the dead. Therefore, the people began to make offerings there."[4]

The Virgin rescues another squire from prison in Cantiga 301. He implores the Virgin to save him from his death sentence. He has always fasted on her holy days and trusted in her mercy. She frees him from his irons and the next thing he knows is he awakens to find himself at her shrine. He must have startled those folks in the church when he suddenly appeared before them in front of the altar holding his irons.

In Cantiga 313, pilgrims sailing from Italy are saved from a storm at sea by the Virgin. They are carrying a precious chalice to Compostela. During the storm they pray to the saints, including Peter, Nicolas, Matthew and James. However, they are ignored by all of the saints. On board is a priest who says he has heard that the Virgin in Villalcázar is good at helping

---

4   Kulp-Hill Kathleen, p. 337.

people in distress. He urges them all to call upon the Virgin, so they all knelt down to pray to her. At that moment a dove as white as snow flew onto the ship and a brilliant light lit up the ship. The weather cleared and the sea became calm. As an offering of thanks the pilgrims gave their precious chalice to the priest to take to the Virgin's Church in Villalcázar. Chalk another one up for the Virgin. Sorry, Saint James.

A woman scorned is the theme of Cantiga 355. A young woman tries to entice a young man who has no interest in her. He wishes to go to the Virgin's shrine in Villalcázar. She wants to accompany him and he flat out tells her he is not interested in her and above all will never marry her. He goes to the shrine to pay homage to the Virgin. Then he buys a stone for the church. On his way home, the young woman plots her revenge. She pretends that she has been raped and beaten by the young man. Funny there is no trial to speak of, the townsmen just listen to her story and the young man is immediately hung. His final prayer is to the Virgin, pleading for his life and reminding her how he spent all his money to buy a stone for her church. The Virgin brings the stone that he purchased and places it under his feet, which saves his life. The next day the people come to take his body down, but see that he is still alive. He now tells them the story of the stone and his version of what happened between him and the girl.

With all these miracles associated with the church in Villalcázar, specifically the shrine of the White Virgin, Alfonso laid a substantial groundwork for attracting the medieval pilgrim to this shrine. It is my hope and intent that today's pilgrim upon reading these stories will be enticed to make a stop at this shrine, too. I hope, too, that if the reader finds the miracles entertaining they will read more of them. They all follow a formulaic structure, which may seem monotonous at times. However, some of them may make you laugh hysterically or just chuckle. Others may even move you to tears. You may even say "what rot" or "what nonsense." At the very least they will give you a touch of life in the middle ages.

Chapter 9

Carrión de los Condes —Debunking The Myth

About three miles (5 km) from Villalcázar is the town of Carrión de los Condes, a town of about ten thousand in the tenth and eleventh centuries, in 2012 it registered a population of just a little over two thousand. During this heyday period it was an important center for royalty and one of the richest towns in the northern area of Spain. The Monastery of San Zoilo, founded in the tenth century, was built by Count Gómez Diaz de Carrión's wife, Teresa. It was her son who was responsible for retrieving the bones of San Zoilo from the Emir of Cordova. Because he offered his services to the Emir in fighting a rival Moorish claimant, the Emir rewarded him by allowing him to take the bones of San Zoilo from Cordova to Carrión. To guard these precious relics, his mother, Teresa, had the monastery built. It exists today as an upscale hotel and houses the tombs of many celebs from ages past, including the Count Gómez and his sons. They have been misrepresented and entangled in the devious deeds attributed to the Count Gonzalo and his sons, the Infantes de Carrión, in the epic poem, "El Cid." It may be due to the fact that the Counts' names seem similar and the Infantes having the added place name of Carrión that causes the confusion between the real persons and the fictitious ones.

In the poem, there are episodes associated with the place, Carrión, and the Conde de Carrión. The episodes include the marriage of the Infantes de Carrión to the Cid's daughters, the lion escaping, the shaming of the Infantes' cowardly behavior, the defilement of the Cid's daughters in the woods near Carrión, and the Cid receiving justice for his daughters' abuse at the hands of their husbands. The *Conde* (*Count*) and the Infantes of Carrión as they appear in the poem are figments of the poet's imagination. First, the title *infante* is misleading. The term can mean heir, prince, scion, lord, or even infant. In reference to the poem, I prefer to use the term *infante*, meaning *lord*, and will refer to the two men as the Infantes with this meaning. The English term "prince" is not suitable since their father is Conde Gonzalo, a count and not a king.

According to the poem, the two Infantes felt shamed by the Cid after the lion incident. What occurred is this: the Cid had fallen asleep and a lion had escaped from his cage. The Cid's men surrounded him so as to protect him as he slept. The two Infantes ran in fright and hid, one behind a wine press and the other in the outhouse. The Cid awoke, leaped to his feet, grabbed the lion by its nape and put him back in his cage.

Mio Çid por sos yernos demand e no falló;
maguer los están llamando, ninguno non responde.
Quando los fallaron, assí vinieron sin color;
non vidiestes tal juego commo iva por la cort;

mandólo vedar mio Çid el Campeador.
Muchos tovieron por enbaídos infantes de Carrión
fiera cosa les pesa desto que les cuntió.[1]

My Cid inquired after his sons-in-law, who couldn't be found;
though they were called for, neither one responded.
When they were found, they were quite pale;
you've never heard such jokes as were circulated through the hall;
My Cid the Champion ordered a stop to them.
The young lords of Carrión
considered themselves gravely offended by what had befallen them.

The Infantes are so mortified by their shame that they plot revenge against the Cid even though he was not the one mocking them.

Meanwhile, the Cid is besieged by Moroccan forces and the Infantes are overheard discussing their chances in battle. They fear their wives will soon be widows if they fight, but at the same time if there is victory and they survive there will be great booty. Having balanced all this, they decide to fight even though the Cid has said they could leave. They insist on leading the charge, but Don Fernán (the name of one of the Infantes) runs away when attacked by a Moor and the Cid's knight, Pedro Bermúdez, kills the Moor for him and allows Don Fernán to have the credit. He also promises not to tell anyone.

After the battle, the Infantes and the Cid's knights get their booty. The knights continue to discuss the battle and praise the bravery of those that performed on the battlefield. They

---

1   Anon, *Poem of My Cid* (Selections) (Mineola, New York: Dover Publications, Edited and Translated by Stanley Appelbaum, 2005), pp. 74–5.

make comments about the two Infantes not being seen in battle and make jokes about it:

Vassallos de mio Çid sediense sonrrisando:
quien lidiara mejor o quien fora en alcanço;
mas non fallavan i a Díago ni a Ferrando.
Por aquestos juegos que ivan levantando,
elas noches e los días tan mal los escarmentando,
tal mal se conssejaron estos iffantes amos.[2]

My Cid's vassals were smiling:
they discussed who had fought best and who had taken part in the pursuit,
but they had not discovered Diego or Fernando in either group.
Because of the jokes they kept telling,
mocking them harshly both night and day,
those two young lords contrived an evil plan.

The evil plan is to revenge themselves through their wives.

Thus, they beg the Cid to let them return with their wives to their home in Carrión. The Cid gives them their leave and off they go. However, the Cid decides to have Félez Muñoz, (a fictional character recorded as the Cid's nephew in the poem) go to Carrión to make sure things are acceptable for his daughters. Muñoz had been ordered to go straight to Carrión "*…mas de so grado non fo. En la Carrera do iva doliól el coraçon,…*" ("*…but he did so unwillingly. On his path his heart misgave him;…*"[3]), so he leaves his party and goes through a dense wood to wait for the Infantes' retinue to pass. However, only the two Infantes pass by where Muñoz

2   Ibid., pp. 84–5.
3   Ibid., pp. 96–7.

has hidden himself. After they pass by, he turns back on their trail and finds the two women barely alive. Muñoz rescues them and gets them to a safe shelter where they are cared for. Later the Cid demands retribution. Since the Infantes have already spent the money given them by the Cid, they have to repay him with personal property and return the Cid's famous swords Tizona and Colada, ones he had given them for what he thought was bravery in battle. Still, the Cid demands more and the king agrees to a battle between the Infantes, their father and three of the Cid's men. The Cid's men win their contests against the two lords and Gonzalo Ansúrez, their father. The three defeated give up as they are about to be killed.

About the only thing that is real in these episodes is the name of the place near where the defilement of the Cid's daughters takes place, that is, Carrión. The Infantes in the poem were from Carrión but their names do not match those found on the tombs in the Monastery of San Zoilo. There we find the name Gómez; not González, as found in the poem. Moreover, scholars have shown that the Infantes of the epic poem (Don Fernán and Don Diego) are not related to the ones that are buried in the Monastery of San Zoilo and that these incidents in the poem only happened in the mind of the poet.

What did happen is that the Cid's daughters actually married nobility, but not the Infantes from Carrión. Cristina (her real name, as opposed to Elvira in the poem) married a prince of Navarre, and María (her real name, as opposed to Sol as stated in the poem) married Ramón

Berenguer III, Count of Barcelona. It would seem highly unlikely that they would marry into royal or noble families if they had been already married and, moreover, defiled in the manner as stated in the poem.

In regards to the town of Carrión, it must be a bit disconcerting for the townsmen of Carrión to hear foreigners speak about their town only in terms of the place where the scoundrels in the epic poem came from. The number of people who write about it as if it were a true fact is astounding, too. There are numerous blogs and articles on the internet that continue to preserve these episodes as historic fact when they are not. I overheard a pilgrim who was visiting the Monastery of San Zoilo and viewing the tombs say, "Why would they bury such evil men in such beautiful tombs as these after what they did to those poor girls?" Why, indeed! I can only hope that more people will become enlightened about the historical facts of this poem before reading the mythical, fictional parts that are recounted as historical happenings. They are told so well that it is often difficult to discern the real truth from the invented truth. However, once the truth is known, the fictional can be accepted as artistic enhancements used by the poet to give his work drama, color, emotion, symbolic meanings etc., the needed elements to create an enticing literary work.

Carrión de los Condes does not owe all of its notoriety to the epic poem of "El Cid." It is also the birthplace of two Spanish poets. One of these is Sem Tob de Carrión (1290–c.1370). He was the first recorded or named Jew to write in Spanish. He wrote *Proverbios Morales* (*Moral Proverbs*), a collection of moralizing maxims. His work is important to

Spanish literature because it sets a standard for later writers of similar works. One curious notion that some scholars have is that Sem Tob was the author of the famous "Danza de la Muerte" ("Dance of Death") poem. It is true that the poem was found in a manuscript immediately following his work, *Proverbios Morales*, but most scholars now believe it was from an unknown French original and not Sem Tob's work, but perhaps a translation.

A poet that admired Sem Tob and wrote proverbial poems is also from Carrión de los Condes, the Marqués de Santillana or Iñigo López de Mendoza (1398–1458). He praises Sem Tob as a great troubadour and a writer of good things. Santillana's proverbial writings are clearly influenced by a European, Spanish source while Sem Tob's are Jewish and Arabic. Santillana writes more than moralistic maxims and is better remembered for introducing the Italian sonnet form into Spanish poetry. However, literary critics appreciate more his simplistic expressions found in his *serranillas* (short poems in Spanish literature that focus on commonplace subjects), where the folkloric combines with fresh exquisite expressions. A sculptured bust of his likeness lies in the plaza in Carrión de los Condes. Here are a few lines from his often-quoted serranilla, "De la Finojosa":

Moça tan fermosa
Non vi ne la frontera,
Como una vaquero
De la Finojosa

Faciendo la vía
Del Calatraveño

A Santa María,
Vencido del sueño,
Por tierra fragosa
Perdí la carrera,
Do vi la vaquera
De la Finojosa[4]

I ne'er on the border
Saw girl fair as Rosa,
The charming milk maiden
Of Sweet Finojosa.

Once making a journey
From Calatraveño
To Santa Maria,
From weary desire
Of sleep, down a valley
I strayed, where young Rosa
I saw, the milk-maiden
Of lone Finojosa.

Santillana is also given credit for having written the first formal literary criticism in Spanish. It is found in his *Proemia* (*Preface*) where he breaks literary style into three classifications: high, middle and low. According to him high should be used for writing in Latin and Greek, middle for formal works in the vernacular language, and low for ballads and songs of a non-formal nature.

One final note on Santillana is that he has a connection with the Condestable, Don Pedro Fernández de Velasco, who is buried in a lavish tomb in the cathedral at Burgos and was

---

4   *Nine Centuries of Spanish Literature* (New York: Dover Publications, Inc. Ed. by Seymour Resnick and Jeanne Pasmantier, 1994), pp. 44–7.

previously mentioned in an earlier chapter. The Condestable's wife, Doña Mencía de Mendoza, was the daughter of Santillana and like her father, was a lover of art and literature.

While the name Carrión de los Condes still conjures up legends of the past, they should only be appreciated as fictional elements used to enhance a literary piece. Moreover, visitors should be aware of this and also of the past residential poets whose noteworthy contributions have left their mark on the town, the country and the world. In addition, the Monastery of San Zoilo with its history and artifacts adds an enriching experience for pilgrims who visit here and are aware of the historical and mythical facts.

Chapter 10

Bits and Pieces

There are many small towns and villages along the way to Santiago that have no other significance than being a part of the pilgrim's walk. Pilgrims do not usually venture a stay in these places mainly because lodgings no longer exist or never existed. They may stop for sustenance if there is a café or bar. In all probability they breeze right through these hamlets without a thought to what wispy tales await them, if only they would inquire. They may never know such towns contain delightful, almost gossipy-type tales certain to please even the most obstinate of listeners. Therefore, for all who speed through the small towns on your pilgrimage (and I know who you are), here are some bits and pieces from these towns for you to enjoy.

Each of these towns have a contribution to give to you, the pilgrim (that's a switch; usually it's the pilgrim doing the contribution). Even if it is only a small contribution, which most of them are, the listener or reader may glean a fact or two that will provide pleasure, entertainment, or something novel. These snippet stories should not overtax your intellect or bore you. So enjoy!

Just outside the town of Sahagún you cross the Río Cea via an old bridge restored from the original Roman construction during the eleventh and sixteenth centuries. You will see a forest after crossing the bridge. This forest is said to be the site of the legend concerning Charlemagne and the field of lances. The tale is told in *PT*, chapter VIII. Here, Charlemagne prepares his army to do a final battle with Aigolandus's army. The night before the battle many of Charlemagne's soldiers thrust their lances upright into the ground. The next morning some of the lances are found to have bark and leaves growing from them. The owners of the lances cut them down, leaving roots from which sprang the groves that are seen today. Believe it or not!

Our next little piece takes us to the town of Mansilla de las Mulas. The name *Mansilla* comes from *mano en silla*, which means *hand on the saddle* (and the symbol of a hand on a saddle is part of the town's coat of arms). The word *mulas* means *mules* and probably relates back to the days when the town was a market for these animals. Our literary piece is a picaresque novel (an authentic Spanish genre), titled *La pícara Justina*, published around 1605, give or take five years, and has much of its setting taking place in Mansilla de las Mulas. The word *pícaro* in the masculine form means *scoundrel* or *rogue*. A female *pícara* might be referred to as *naughty* or *mischievous* and always one who lived by her wits, along with deceit and thievery. The first translation of this book into English was *The Country Jilt*. In this picaresque novel the chief protagonist is a woman. This seventeenth-century novel's main character, Justina, evolved from a rich literary tradition going back to

Fernando de Rojas's character, Celestina, from his work, *La Celestina* of 1499. Justina carries the same bawdy traits of Celestina and lays the way for other female pícaras such as Moll Flanders in the eighteenth-century novel of the same name by Daniel Defoe. Most of the more popular Spanish picaresque novels have a male as the chief protagonist. This particular novel captures the environs of Mansilla de las Mulas for the setting of many passages in the novel. What remains to be said is that the authorship of this novel is up for grabs. Some attribute it to Francisco López de Úbeda and others to Andrés Pérez. Still others maintain that Andrés Pérez used the name of Francisco López de Úbeda as a pseudonym.

Somehow the point of its authorship seems trivial. What is significant is that this genre had a great influence on the rest of world literature. Some examples would be Fielding's *Tom Jones* or Twain's *Huckleberry Finn*. Beginning in 1554 with the picaresque novel, *La vida de Lazarillo de Tormes y de sus fortunas y adversidades* (*The Life of Lazarillo de Tormes and of His Fortunes and Adversities*) (authorship also up for grabs) these novels became quite popular and were often put on the Church's dreaded *Index of Prohibited Works* because of their satirical criticism against the Church and crown. At any rate, *La pícara Justina* and its setting in Mansilla de las Mulas continued its influence on twentieth-century Spain in that Spanish television created a series titled *Las pícaras*. This very popular TV series of the 1980s recreated picaresque works of the seventeenth century, including those by Cervantes and episodes from *La pícara Justina*. Most of these picaresque works have been translated into English offering readers light and sometimes hilarious reading.

La pícara Justina is divided into four books and like most of the other picaresque novels is narrated by the protagonist. In this case it is Justina. Book I starts with a history of her lineage and ends with the death of her parents, which is somewhat grotesquely detailed. Her father's ears are eaten by the family dog as the body awaits burial. Her mother chokes to death engorging herself on a rather long piece of sausage that is described as half a yard long and hanging out of her mouth. She dies while people are trying to pull it out of her mouth. (Too bad that the Heimlich maneuver did not exist back then.) The remaining books describe Justina's devious maneuvers to gain material goods and improve her social status via trickery or thievery. Throughout the books, the author pokes fun at the clergy and the nobility through his main character.

Book II is titled *La pícara romera* (*The Wily Pilgrim*) in which Justina declares that she likes to have a good time either dancing or attending pilgrimages. Justina's idea of a pilgrimage is traveling to a town that is celebrating a religious feast day and joining in the festivities by dancing, drinking; and pilfering intoxicated attendees. There is not much emphasis on the religious aspect of her "pilgrimages."

The fourth book ends with Justina getting married, several times in fact. Most of her marriages end in disaster. Her main objective in marrying is to improve her social standing. The irony of this is that her final marriage is to a man named Guzmán de Alfarache who just happens to have the same name of the title and protagonist of an earlier picaresque novel (1599). It is almost certain that this character being so named is no accident in *La pícara Justina*, but was used to show that Justina would never escape her station in life. Especially with

Guzmán now her husband, they both will always be pícaros engendering more pícaros.

Leaving Mansilla de las Mulas we walk a few kilometers to the tiny village of Villaverde de Sandoval, where it is said a soldier returned home after years of imprisonment by the Moors. He disguised himself as a pilgrim on his way home. While he was gone, his wife spent her days doing charitable works at the nearby monastery. One of the things she did was to perform the ritual of washing the feet of returning pilgrims. One day she was washing the feet of a pilgrim and she gasped in surprise. She recognized the feet of her husband who had stopped at the monastery before going home. There is no mention that his feet had any distinguishing features, such as a deformity or an ugly hairy mole. All I can say is, if this woman recognized her husband's feet and not his face, he must have had the best cared for feet in Spain.

As you make your way to the city of León it is noteworthy to mention the Basilica of San Isidoro (Saint Isidore) (c. 560–636), even though this saint really belongs to Seville because he grew up in Seville and is its patron saint. His remains end up in León due to the fact that Seville was under control of the Moors in the eleventh century. An agreement made with Abbad II al-Mu'tadid, the Muslim ruler of Seville, allowed for Isidore's relics to be brought to León where they could be buried on Christian soil. His fame not only lies with his work for the Church, but also for his erudite writings. His most famous work is his *Etymologiae* (*Etymologies*), which stands as the first known encyclopedia in western history. Almost as soon as he finished it, the *Etymologiae* became the most sought-after reference work throughout medieval Europe and continued so for the next nine centuries. Here is a sample of what a student could find if he needed to look up information on divine and human laws:

All laws are either divine or human. The divine are established by nature, the human by customs. Therefore the latter vary, since different laws please different people. Divine law is fas, human law is jus. It is fas to pass through another's property, but it is not jus.[1]

What did Saint Isidore have to say about Saint James? Not much is known and, besides, the legend of Saint James was in its infancy when Isidore was alive. His work, <u>Etymologiae</u>, repeats what is told of James's life in the bible. He is not linked to Spain in any way. However, in one of Isidore's other works, *De ortu et obitu patrum*, which is a list of deaths and burials of patriarchs and apostles, there are two short affirmations that James went to Spain. That he was buried there is not affirmed. In addition, there is some debate on whether Isidore is even the author of this work. In spite of this, it is still relevant that Isidore or some unknown author of the early Middle Ages affirms James's presence in Spain.

As you leave León on foot via the Camino you will pass by the *Parque de Quevedo (Quevedo's Park)* named in memory of the seventeenth-century Spanish poet and writer. He was not born in this city, but he so incensed many of the nobility with his satiric and acerbic writings that he was thrown in prison here for four years. Because he was a knight of the

---

1 Saint Isidore, *Isidore of Seville's Etymologies: the complete English translation of Isidori Hispalensis Episcopi Etymologiarum sive Originum Libri xx* (Charlotte, Vermont, trans. by Pricilla Throop, Vol. 1, Books I–X, 2005), Book V, Section II.

Order Santiago, he was allowed to stay at the Monastery of San Marcos in León, which was run by the military Order of Santiago. Even under these conditions, his stay was anything but pleasant. He tells how nobody spoke to him for two years. In prison, Quevedo spent much of his time reading and writing. Writing to his friend, Adán de la Parra, he depicts his prison life hour by hour. "From ten to eleven, I spend my time in prayer and devotions, and from eleven to noon I read good and bad authors; because there is no book, despicable as it can be, that does not contain something good…"[2]

Upon his release from prison he was exiled to his familial village and died shortly thereafter in 1645. One of the most quoted poems is his "Don Dinero" ("Lord of Dollars" or "Don Money"). Here are a few lines:

Don Dinero

Poderoso caballero
Es don Dinero.
Madre, yo al oro me humillo,
Él es mi amante y mi amado,
Pues de puro enamorado
Anda continuo amarillo.
Que pues doblón o sencillo
Hace todo cuanto quiero,
Poderoso caballero
Es don Dinero.
Nace en las Indias honrado,
Donde el mundo le acompaña;
Viene a morir en España,

---

2 Francisco de Quevedo y Villegas, *Obras de Don Francisco de Quevedo Villegas* (Madrid: M. Rivadeneyra, 1859), p. 590.

Y es en Génova enterrado.
Y pues quien le trae al lado
Es hermoso, aunque sea fiero,
Poderoso caballero
Es don Dinero.[3]

The Lord of Dollars

Over kings and priests and scholars
Rules the mighty Lord of Dollars.
Mother, unto gold I yield me,
He and I are ardent lovers;
Pure affection now discovers
How his sunny rays shall shield me!
For a trifle more or less
All his power will confess,
Over kings and priest and scholars
Rules the mighty Lord of Dollars.
In the Indies did they nurse him,
While the world stood round admiring;
And in Spain was his expiring;
And in Genoa did they hearse him;
And the ugliest at his side
Shines with all of beauty's pride;
Over kings and priest and scholars
Rules the mighty Lord of Dollars.

Quevedo not only excelled in poetry but also was successful with the picaresque novel. His work, *La vida del Buscón* (*The Life of the Swindler*) is a good read and takes the picaresque genre to a new level of excellence. You will not be bored and there are sure to be some laughing moments.

---

3   Resnick and Pasmantier, pp. 230–1.

However, some women may find his stinging remarks about them insulting and degrading. Just remember the period in which this was written (1608). This is not my favorite quote in the work, but it does depict the scorn and treatment of women by the protagonist, Pablo, and lets you know what a scoundrel he truly is:

…pero como yo no quiero las mujeres para consejeras ni bufinas, sino para acostarme con ellas, y si son feas y discretas es lo mismo que acostarse con Aristóteles o Séneca o con un libro, procúrolas de buenas partes para el arte de las ofensas[4]

…still, as I don't need women to give me advice or make me laugh but just to go to bed with—if they're ugly and intelligent I might just as well be in bed with Aristotle or Seneca or a book—I usually pick them as being good for a roll in the hay.[5]

In retort to his ideas on women, I say curling up with a good book is sometimes more desirable than a mediocre man.

Quevedo had a close tie to Saint James. When debates were being held to change Spain's patron saint, Saint James, to Saint Teresa of Ávila, Quevedo stood up for Saint James. He argued that Teresa being a woman and virgin could not go into battle. Spaniards were warriors and conquered with the help of a warrior saint. I wonder what Quevedo would have argued if the Virgin Mary had been nominated for patron saint. She is considered to be superior to Saint James. I also wonder why

---

4   Francisco de Quevedo, *El Buscón* (Madrid: Lável Artes Gráficas, 2011), p. 174.

5   Francisco de Quevedo, *Two Spanish Picaresque Novels (Lazarillo de Tormes and The Swindler)* (London: Penguin Books, translated by Michael Alpert, 1988), p. 188.

no one mentioned Saint Joan of Arc's feats as a rebuttal to the female warrior argument. Nevertheless, Quevedo's side won and Saint James is still considered the patron saint of Spain.

Leaving León you soon come upon the church of *La Virgen del Camino* (*The Virgin of the Way*). The legend connected to this church is that a shepherd had a vision of the Virgin who told him to throw a stone. Wherever the stone landed he was to build a church. The church drew many people because of the numerous miracles that were said to have occurred here. Thus, the church became a side pilgrimage on the way to Santiago.

Farther down the road about twenty-one miles (35 km) is the town, Hospital de Óbrigo, with its famous historical bridge. It is one of the longest medieval bridges and was constructed over a previous Roman bridge. You cross over the bridge and river of the same name, Óbrigo, by way of *Paso Honroso* (*Passage of Honor*), which is the link to its historic past.

According to legend, in the year 1434, Don Suero de Quiñones, a knight from León, was infatuated with a woman who had scorned him. He put an iron collar around his neck to show he was bound to her. When this did not impress her, he felt he had been disgraced. To regain his honor, he got the king to consent to twenty-two conditions of challenge and had them sent to the best knights in the land. The king was so agreeable that he sent out heralds to announce the twenty-two conditions of challenge across the land. The date of the tournament was set for July 11th. As luck would have it, not only did the feast of Saint James fall in July, it was a holy year for the feast of Saint James in 1434. (A holy year is any year in which the saint's feast falls on a Sunday.) This meant there would be lots of traffic coming through Óbrigo during the upcoming jousting tournament. The jousting endured for several weeks and there was always a banquet afterwards on the riverbank.

On July 15, Suero met a Catalan challenger. This challenger had heard of Suero's status so he donned himself in an extra layer of steel. Making fun of him, Suero clothed himself in light armor covered by a woman's blouse. The Catalan became enraged at this and suddenly struck a blow that knocked Suero from his horse. The crowd gasped and feared for Suero's wellbeing. A moment later, Suero jumped up and said it was nothing. The crowd relaxed and continued enjoying the joust.

On July 20, Suero and his men defeated nine knights who were on their way to Santiago de Compostela. On the last day of the tournament, August 9, Suero declared himself free since he had proved himself to the lady in question by wearing the iron neckband and breaking three hundred lances at the tournament. He took off the neckband and gave it to the judges. The crowd endorsed the action by their loud shouts of approval. Then the attendees celebrated with a procession from the bridge all the way to León.

Now that he was free, Suero said he would make a pilgrimage to Santiago. He did such a pilgrimage and when he reached Santiago, he left his arms and a gold collar or choker-like necklace at the cathedral as a symbol of his release as a prisoner of love. Pilgrims today can see the gold collar with gems of pearls and an emerald that was added at the end of the fourteenth century in the *Capilla de las reliquias* (*Chapel of the Relics*). It is on the bust of *Santiago Alfeo* (*Saint James The*

Less or Lesser). He was also one of the twelve apostles, who like the patron saint of Spain, was named James. To distinguish one from the other both were given monikers. Santiago, the patron saint of Spain, had the moniker, *The Great or Greater*.

Moving on, we pass through many towns before reaching Villafranca del Bierzo, which roughly translates as *French town in a mountainous area*. Here a young woman named, María de Toledo y Osorio, lived in the early seventeenth century with her father, the Marqués de Villafranca. María not only left us a story, but also a seventeenth-century convent built just for her. One might call this story, "The Nun's Tale".

According to the story, her father had arranged a marriage for his daughter, but she refused to marry. She wanted to dedicate her life to God and join a nunnery. Her father was furious with this idea, so he locked her up in the castle. Being ever so determined to fulfill her dream of becoming a nun, María escaped from the castle by climbing down a rope that she had made from bed sheets. She entered a convent and took her vows. However, her father had the so-called last word. He said if she must be a nun, she would be the prioress or mother superior. Thus, her father built her a convent, *Convento de la Anunciada* (*Convent of the Annunciation*), which she headed from 1608 until her death in 1631. As a nun she must have also had time to write some poetry for she is said to have "… won modest fame as a poetess."[6] I would have liked to have read some of her poetry, but was unable to find any of her works in publication. So much for her renown! (If any of

---

6   Gitlitz and Davidson, p. 300.

you readers have ever seen her poetry, I would love to hear from you. My email can be found in the section called "About the Author" at the end of this book.)

Entering the province of Galicia via the Camino, the first significant town is O'Cebreiro. Most pilgrims stop here to pay homage to Father Elías Valiña Sampedro. The results of his tireless efforts from the early 1960s till his death in 1989 in promoting the Camino are seen today in the increased number of pilgrims and the numerous pilgrim lodgings built during his lifetime. In addition, Father Valiña wrote books about the Camino, one of which was the first modern guidebook for the pilgrimage. Father Sampedro died in 1989 but lived to see his beloved Camino declared a world heritage site in 1987.

Pilgrims also visit the parish church in O'Cebreiro to see where an unusual miracle took place and view the chalice involved. The miracle concerns a peasant of the fourteenth century who trudged through a heavy snowstorm to hear mass at this church. Just as the priest was consecrating the host the peasant entered the church. The priest scolded him for coming so far in the snowstorm for just a bit of bread and sip of wine. At that very moment the bread and wine became flesh and blood. Pope Innocent VIII authenticated the miracle, and it has been immortalized in various media such as poetry, paintings and sculpture. Moreover, the chalice and contents of this miracle are on display in the church in a reliquary. Some writers claim that the Holy Grail was hidden in O'Cebreiro and that the chalice in the miracle is the Holy Grail. There is no evidence that this chalice was the chalice used at Christ's last supper. However, the miracle did become part of the town's emblem or coat of arms, which remains as a reference to the miracle that took place there centuries ago.

As legend would have it there is a second part to this miracle that concerns a queen from Portugal. She arrived at the monastery and was told of the miracle, which she did not believe. She continued on her journey only to be thrown by her horse. Her entourage carried her back to the monastery where she was cared for. She spent several days there and recuperated nicely. In thanks for her care, she gave the monastery a jeweled chalice in which to put the wine/blood of the miracle. Every year thereafter on the anniversary of the miracle the wine turned into the blood of Christ.

The last important stop before reaching Santiago is *Monte de Gozo* (*Mount Joy*). Pilgrims stop here to view the cathedral spires of Santiago de Compostela, which are about three miles (5 km) away. There is also a monument that was built to commemorate the visit of Pope John Paul II, who celebrated mass here in August 1989 for World Youth Day. The sculptured monument depicts, among other things, Pope John Paul embracing Saint James from the saint's backside as pilgrims traditionally do in the cathedral. Another side depicts the image of Saint Francis of Assisi, who is said to have made the pilgrimage in the early thirteenth century.

Monte de Gozo is also the area where Saint James is said to have carried two men, one dead and the other alive. The full story found in Book II of the *Codex*, Miracle 4, states that thirty war heroes from Lorraine decided to visit Saint James's tomb. They make a vow to assist each other, if the need arises. However, one of the group members does not wish to be encumbered with such a vow. Nevertheless, they all set out together on the journey. It happens that one of the men becomes ill and cannot make it by himself. Because of the sworn oath, the others carry him, which causes them a lot of work and time. What normally would have been a five-day journey to the Cize Pass for foot soldiers takes them fifteen days and they have horses.

The men become so fatigued that they abandon the sick man. The man who did not take the oath is the one who remains with him. He cares for the man and stays with him, but unfortunately the sick man dies. Now his caretaker is at a loss as how to bury him. There is no place in this area for a decent burial site. Since he can find no one to help him he prays to Saint James. Saint James arrives dressed as a soldier on a horse and helps the man by placing both of them on his horse with him. The dead man sits facing Saint James while his caretaker sits behind the saint.

The three of them cross a distance that would comprise a twelve-day journey in one night. At daybreak they arrive at Monte de Gozo, where James tells the soldier to ask the clergy at Santiago de Compostela to bury his pilgrim. James further tells him that after he has seen to the burial he should start home. He tells him he will meet his former group of friends in León on his return trip. James orders him to tell them that God is displeased with them for breaking their vow and abandoning their friend. In addition he orders that they should repent and do penance, otherwise their pilgrimage is for naught. Upon hearing this, the soldier realizes that he has been with Saint James. He wants to fall at his feet but the saint is no longer visible.

The soldier makes his way to León where the other

soldiers have stopped. He relates to them all that has happened and what Saint James wanted them to know. The soldiers receive penance on the spot from no less than the bishop of León himself. The men complete their pilgrimage and the story ends by stating a moral dictum: "If there is something to be established by this miracle, it is that whatever is vowed to God must be fulfilled with joy, inasmuch as someone fulfilling worthy vows obtains forgiveness from the Lord."[7]

In relating the legends of Saint James's burial in Spain, the queen of Iria Flavia (Iria Flavia is the Roman name and Padrón is the Spanish name of the town) appears in several versions of the legend. Before I relate her role in James's story, allow me to tell you one that will give you a good idea of her temperament. First of all, her name is *Lupa*, which means *she-wolf*. She was the Leona Helmsley[8] of her day, and like Leona, she could just have well have been called the "Queen of Mean" because of how she lived and behaved. In this story she lives in a cave on a hillside. One day a young lad is bringing his pigs to feed in the hills. He notices how some of the pigs are increasing in weight faster than some of the others. He decides to follow them and that is when he encounters Lupa who tells him that she will make sure all his pigs become very fat if he will give her the best of the sausages at slaughter time. The boy is delighted to do so.

---

7   Coffey, et al., p. 68

8   For those of you who are unfamiliar with Leona Helmsley, she was a very wealthy hotel owner who ruled her employees like a tyrant. She earned her reputation by publicly degrading them. She spent time in prison for tax fraud, died in 2007, and left most of her millions to her dog, leaving her grandchildren without a cent.

Slaughter time arrives and the boy's guardian finds out about the deal between Lupa and the boy. Now the guardian is a very stingy old woman. She gives Lupa some bad sausages and Lupa becomes enraged and assures the old woman that she will receive an exemplary punishment. At that very moment, the sausages turn into snakes and devour the old woman. Legend has it that you can still see her skeleton in the bottom of the well that stands near the cave.

Now that you know what kind of person Lupa is we can begin with how James's body returned to Spain. One of the versions tells how James's disciples arrived with his body by sea and landed at Galicia near Padrón. His disciples laid his body on a stone that immediately softened like wax and shaped itself into a sarcophagus that fit his body. They then met Queen Lupa and told her of their sea voyage and asked her to give them a place to bury James. She cunningly sends them off to the King of Duio, who is known to be very cruel also. The king listens to their story and schemes to entrap them and kill them, but the disciples find out about the scheme and flee before he can carry out his plan.

In another version the disciples are thrown in prison and an angel sets them free. But in both versions the king sends troops after them. They come to a river where they must cross a bridge. The disciples make it across, but the bridge collapses when the troops cross and they all drown. (Does this sound slightly familiar to the biblical "parting of the sea" story in "*Exodus*?") When the king finds out the disciples were trying to bury Saint James, he repents out of fear and sends soldiers out to find the disciples. He promises if they return he will give them anything they want. The disciples do go back and convert the whole city.

When they return to see Lupa, they inform her of the king's actions and resulting conversion. The queen is very upset over this and plans another devious scheme to try and undo the disciples. She tells them that she has some oxen in a mountainous place that they can use to carry James's body to wherever they want and build his tomb. Now Lupa knows that the oxen are anything but tame and gentle. They are, in fact, wild savage bulls. She is hoping the disciples will be torn apart by these creatures.

The disciples are unaware of her trickery and go up into the mountain where they encounter a fire-breathing dragon. They hold a cross in front of him and his belly explodes in half. The disciples give thanks for their deliverance and change the name of that spot from *El Monte Ilicino* to *Pico Sacro*. El Monte Ilicino was said to be the residence of devils and a place where people were seduced into the rites of devil worship. The disciples exorcised the place and now it is known as *Pico Sacro* or *Sacred Peak*.

After getting rid of the dragon they bless the bulls, who then become gentle as lambs. They yoke the bulls and without anyone guiding them they take the body straight into the queen's palace. The queen is somewhat distressed upon seeing this and immediately converts to Christianity. Not only does she convert, but she also changes her palace into a church for Saint James, which she endows generously. She spends the rest of her life doing good works. Two of the disciples guard the tomb of Saint James until their death. Both were said to be buried next to James as well as being next to him in heaven. Queen Lupa is said to be buried in a granite tomb without any decoration or lettering, but with the other ruling kings of that area.

One of the most neglected writers of this same area, until recently, was the nineteenth-century poetess, Rosalía de Castro (1837–1885). Not until late in the twentieth century did she begin to receive recognition for her works. Most scholars say this was due to Franco's insistence that everything had to be written in Castilian, and most of Castro's works were in the Galician dialect and, therefore, not very visible. This may have been true in the twentieth century when Franco was in power and her works were suppressed due to the dialect they were written in, but she wrote and lived in the nineteenth century. Her works were not promoted then as some scholars believe because she was a woman from a lower class and most of her critics were powerful aristocrats. Whatever the reason, she has left some beautiful creations about her native province and her struggles with her faith and everyday life. She wrote about the local scenery, the land, the people, poverty and survival, especially that of women and the men who were forced to migrate because of it.

De Castro was quite familiar with Santiago and its cathedral. One of the poems that she wrote is called "Na Catredal" ("In the Cathedral"). It is from her book of poems titled *Follas Novas* (*New Leaves*) and is in her native Galician dialect. In her description of the Cathedral de Santiago, we get a sense of its majestic grandeur. Here are a few lines from the poem:

O sol poninete, polas vidreiras
de Soledade, lanza serenos
raios, que firen descoloridos

da Groria os ánxeies i o Padre Eterno.
Santos e apóstoles, ¡védeos!, parecen
que os labios moven, que falan quedoto
os uns cos outros,…
¿Estarán vivos?, ¿serán de pedra
aqués sembrantes tan verdadeiros,
aquelas túnicas marabillosas,
aqueles ollos de vida cheos?[9]

The setting sun through stained-glass windows
of Our Lady of Solitude, casts serene
streams, that palely wound
the angels in Heaven and the Eternal Father.
Saints and apostles, look at them!, they seem
move their lips, to speak softly
among themselves,…
Are they alive?, are they made of stone
these faces that are so real,
those splendid tunics,
those eyes full of animation?

In this description she continues and says, "Aquí está a Groria" ("Here is heaven").[10] Then she suddenly switches her mood to one of fear, seeing, "almas tristes dos condanados onde as devoran tódolos demos" ("sad souls of the condemned devoured by every demon").[11] This change in mood is said to be a reflection of her life. She begins to question why God would allow the suffering of the lower classes and also to some

9   Rosalía de Castro, *The Poetry and Prose of Rosalía de* Castro (Lewiston, New York: The Edwin Mellen Press, trans. by Aileen Dever and John P. Dever, 2010), pp. 223–4.

10   Ibid.

11   Ibid., pp. 225–6.

extent, his existence. The cathedral, "for so many years was a place where her heart and mind were at peace but now she feels only anxiety and fear…"[12]

Her personal life was filled with tragedy and struggle. She endured discrimination because of her gender and liberal thinking; and the fact that she was an illegitimate child who had a priest for her father did not help matters. When her father died he left everything to his niece and failed even to mention her in his will. Rosalia had seven children, one died at birth and another at less than a year old. She herself died a very painful death from uterine cancer at the early age of forty-eight.

Her husband was supportive of her writing and was instrumental in getting some of her works published. She mingled with notable writers and poets of her day, including Bécquer, Aguirre and Pondal. She is said to have influenced later Spanish poets such as Federico García Lorca. In contrast, she also felt the sting of other writers of her day such as Emilia Pardo Bazán.

Scholars such as Catherine Davies and Aileen and John Dever believe that Bazán was to some extent responsible for de Castro's literary struggle.[13] Bazán, unlike de Castro, was conservative and had no use for the Galician dialect for serious literary works. Bazán was also a respected literary critic, except for the opinion of Rosalía's husband, Manuel Murguía. He was Bazán's bitter adversary because of the contempt with which she treated Rosalía. Interestingly Rosalía

12   Ibid., Poem 17, p. 440.
13   Ibid., p. 14.

and Emilia are distantly related but were apparently unaware of it, and "kissing cousins" they were not.

Pilgrims and tourists alike visit Rosalía's house in Padrón. It was converted into a museum and is today the headquarters for the Rosalía de Castro Foundation. There is also the familiar pilgrim marker in Santiago along the route that depicts the sculptured head of Rosalía superimposed on the scallop shell.

As previously mentioned, the writer, Emilia Pardo Bazán, was from Galicia and was also intimate with the city of Santiago. She knew and wrote about its pilgrimage traditions. Included in her prolific works are novels, poems, short stories, and articles for newspapers and periodicals. Three of her short stories "El Peregrino" ("The Pilgrim"), "El Caballo Blanco" ("The White Horse") and "La Danza del Peregrino" ("The Pilgrim's Dance") connect in some way to Santiago and/or the pilgrimage. In two of her novels there is focus on Saint James. Her novel, *Pascual López, autobiografía de un estudiante de medicina* (*Pascual López, Autobiography of a Medical Student*) is set in Santiago and makes reference to the legends of Saint James.[14] In *La última fada* (*The Last Fairy*), Saint James is seen in his role as Moor-slayer.[15] However, it is her short story, "The Pilgrim's Dance," that captures the flavor and setting of another era in the present. Her description of the Cathedral of Santiago and even more the pilgrim himself carries the reader back through time without having left the present setting.

---

14   Maryjane Dunn, "Nationalism, Regionalism and Faith in the Works of Emilia Pardo Bazán: St. James and the Pilgrimage to Santiago de Compostela, 1880–1920," *Ad Limina* Vol. 4, No. 4, 2013, p.18.

15   Ibid.

Here we have her describing the rites of the State's yearly *ofrenda* (*offering*) to Santiago as practiced and instituted by Philip the IV in the seventeenth century:

…el colosal incensario vuela como un ave de fuego, encandiladas sus brasas por el vuelo mismo, y vierte nubes de incienso que neutralizan el vaho humano de tanta gente rústica apiñada en la nave, había algo que atrajo mi atención más que el cardenal con sus suntuosas vestiduras pontificales, más que las larguísimas caudas de los caballeros santiaguistas, majestuosamente arrastradas por la alfombra del presbiterio.[16]

…the colossal censer flies above like a firebird, its embers glowing throughout its flight, while pouring out clouds of fragranced incense which neutralizes the steamy stench of so many rustic people jammed into the nave, there was something that attracted my attention, more than the Cardinal with his sumptuous pontifical vestments, more than the very long lines of the Knights of Saint James moving majestically over the altar's carpet. (Translation mine.)

It is the continuance of these rituals along with the description of the cathedral and the physique and dress of the pilgrim that fuses the present and past to become the same time period. The pilgrim is in a state of ecstasy while watching the ceremony. He is wearing the typical pilgrim garb of the Middle Ages with his oilskin cape, staff with scallop shell and his gourd for holding water. The narrator in the story thinks she is having a vision of a pilgrim from the Middle Ages. Being in the cathedral only adds to this vision since most of its structures are from that era.

When the State finishes with its ceremonial offering, the

---

16   Emilia Pardo Bazán, "La danza del peregrino", *Boletín de la Asociación Gaditana del Camino de Santiago,* Núm. 8, enero 2011, p. 8.

festivities begin. People dressed as giants and wearing very large heads enter the scene in front of the altar to begin their dance, a dance that springs from ancient times and rituals. Here the narrator notices how the pilgrim wants to dance like those pilgrims in earlier times. However, he refrains, which she takes as a sign that the spiritualism of the pilgrimage no longer exists as it did in the early days. It may be repressed, since the desire to dance is still seen in the pilgrim's face but no one in the cathedral will dance today with these gigantic actors.

Some scholars see this story as a kind of allegory for Spain and her spirit after the loss of her colonies in 1898.[17] With her defeat in the Spanish American War, she still existed as a nation, but her spirit was deeply subdued, unable to perform a celebratory dance.

---

17   Ibid., pp. 19, 31, 37.

Chapter 11

Missionary-Pilgrim and Matamoros

Most of the art media linked to Saint James depict him as a pilgrim or warrior. Some also depict him as Christ's apostle and missionary. So too, do the legends and myths that are recorded or orally repeated throughout the ages. This dichotomy of his character seems puzzling. It is somewhat like the Roman two-faced god, Janus, who ruled over the beginning and ending of battles, or war and peace. The stark contrasts are actually parts that complete the total character just as Saint James's two faces of pilgrim and warrior complete his. However, it is not my purpose to discuss this in any detail but only to point out the contrasts in his character, their compatibility, and move on to those stories dealing with these different personalities linked to Saint James. (For an in depth study of this topic see John K. Moore, Jr.'s article.[1])

---

1   John K. Moore, Jr., "Juxtaposing James the Greater: Interpreting the Interstices of Santiago as Peregrino and Matamoros," *Project Muse*, University of Alabama at Birmingham. Mervyn H. Sterne Library, 2010.

We have heard some of the legends of Saint James who appears as a pilgrim and seen his image as a pilgrim along the Camino in sculptures. We leave Santiago and head to a nearby town that stands out as the legendary arrival spot of Saint James's body from Jerusalem after his martyrdom in 44 A.D. That spot is the small coastal town of Padrón about sixteen miles (27 km) southwest of Santiago de Compostela. Many pilgrims travel on after Santiago to this site to visit the sacred places linked to Saint James. In Saint James's day, the town was known by its Roman name, Iria Flavia.

In addition to the legend of Saint James's body arriving at Padrón, there are a couple of other legends. One concerns how Saint James would retreat to a rocky hill when he was in danger of being stoned by the local pagans. There were many caves found here and James would seek refuge in them. In one, it is said he blocked it with a huge boulder to prevent the pagans from entering. This particular cave became known as *Peña de Santiago* (*Saint James's Rock*). It was also said that pilgrims entered the cave to receive redemption for their sins.

Another rock that sits near the current hermitage displays two distinct human forms. According to the story, they are of Saint James and an old woman. As the story goes, Saint James was sitting on the hillside and an old woman was passing by. Saint James called to her and asked her to sit with him. While they were seated he spoke to her of Christ and his teachings. She converted to Christianity. During their conversation the two sat next to a huge rock where they left impression of their bodily forms. The rock shows that one of the forms is taller than the other; the taller is said to be Saint James and the shorter, the old woman. Many couples also come to this hillside to sit among the rocks invoking the saint's help in having a child.

Still another story related to Saint James's sanctuary on this hill is that this is the place where he would often celebrate mass and meditate. From the spot where he celebrated mass an altar was built over a spring that Saint James created via a miracle. The miracle happened one day after James had been meditating for several hours. Saint James was very thirsty and some pagans noticing this, challenged him to call upon his god. They said if his god was as great and powerful as he preached, then his god would provide him with water. James invoked Jesus's name and struck the rock with his crosier. Immediately a spring of crystal clear water started to flow and is still flowing today. Pilgrims flock here to drink the water in hopes they will be cured of their various ailments. It is reported that the rate of cures for fever is very high. I am not surprised at this since the waters are ice cold.

A little ways up the coast from Padrón is the town of Muxía (59 miles or 35.5 km), where pilgrims tend to take a side trip while doing Finisterre or Padrón in order to visit places where Saint James was said to have been. One of the stories linked to Muxía is how the Virgin encouraged Saint James.

Saint James was feeling dejected by the townspeople and was about to give up and go home to Jerusalem. He was near the shore and saw a stone boat approaching. What a miraculous boat it must have been since it was made of stone, had a stone mainsail and was navigated by angels. When the boat docked the angels carried Mary through the air to shore. She talked to James and encouraged him to continue his preaching. When she left, James saw that the same angles carried her toward the East. Mary's boat remained in Muxía and James continued his "pilgrimage" of preaching and converting throughout Galicia.

Today pilgrims come to look at three rocks that legend says are three parts of Mary's boat: the hull, the mainsail and the rudder. According to legend, the large rocking stone, which you can touch, is known as *Pedra de Abalar* (*Stone Hull*), was the hull of the Virgin's boat. The other two large stones whose names are the *Pedra dos Cadrís* (*Stone Mainsail*) and the *Pedra do Temón* (*Stone Rudder*) represent the mainsail and rudder.

Pilgrims used to be able to visit the church that stood near these stones, *Our Lady of the Boat* (*Nuestra Señora de la Barca*). On December 25, 2013, lightning struck and destroyed the church. The church was built in the seventeenth century, with modifications in the nineteenth century. I feel fortunate to have been able to visit this church shortly before its destruction and sincerely hope that it will be restored soon. Sources have told me restoration is underway, but you can only view the church from the outside. No completion date for restoring the church was available.

The coastline is one of the deadliest for ships and fishing boats. Not only is the coastline a deadly siren's lair, but it is also a place where the weather has to be constantly watched when fishing or sailing. The coast got the name, *Costa da Morte*, (*Coast of Death*) because of deadly hidden rocks, weather conditions and most of all for the number of shipwrecks that have occurred over the centuries. The list of wrecks is over five hundred.

When the church still existed, it displayed models of

ships that had wrecked on this coast. The ship models hung from the ceiling and these models ranged from galleons and clippers to modern-day battleships. Hopefully it will be restored to its former beauty along with its history of the ships that were wrecked along this coast.

After Saint James's martyrdom in 44 A.D., we do not hear about him until the eleventh century when the legend of the Battle of Clavijo was beginning to spread through a historical document composed by a canon at Compostela named Pedro Marcio.[2] This document, said to be a falsification of the events described therein, contained the sworn oath of King Ramiro, his heirs and the people of Galicia to give a yearly offering to Saint James of Compostela. This is the pseudo-historical origin of the national offering that still continues today. The actual institution of the offering did not happen until much later.

Ramiro was the king involved in the Clavijo battle. He went to battle the Moors because he refused to pay them the one hundred virgins they demanded as a yearly tribute in order to avoid war. Who wouldn't go to war for that price? Besides, where was he going to find ten virgins let alone a hundred?

On the first day of the battle, the Christians suffer a terrible defeat. On the eve before the second battle Ramiro has a dream in which Saint James appears and tells him he will aid him in the battle. He even tells him how he will appear,

2   Nicolás Cabrillana Ciézar, "Santiago Matamoros, Historia e Imagen," *Collección: Monografías*, No. 14 (Málaga: Servicio de Publicaciones Diputación de Málaga, 1999), p. 15.

that is, dressed in white, riding a white charger, and carrying a sword and banner. Saint James shows up at the battle and kills seventy thousand Moors. This depiction of Saint James is the basis for his moniker, *Moor Slayer (Matamoros)*. To understand the significance of this forged document spreading this legend and image of Saint James, you only have to observe the thousands of pieces of art and architecture that were engendered from it throughout not only Spain but Europe and the Americas. We not only get Santiago Matamoros but later in the Americas, *Santiago Mataindios (Saint James the Indian Slayer)* and during the wars of independence from Spain, Santiago Mataespañoles (*Saint James the Spaniard Slayer*). It seems a bit ironic to have Saint James fighting against the Spaniards when he has been their patron saint and leader in battles for centuries. It must have been a bit disconcerting to hear their enemies shout out Saint James's name for aid while engaging them in battle. See the work by Nicolás Cabrillana Ciézar for in-depth details on Santiago Matamoros.[3]

Why a clergyman would write a forgery on this event is open for debate, but most scholars believe it probably was due to political, religious and economic necessity.[4] In the document is found also the source of Spain's battle cry. Marcio wrote, "¡Que Dios nos ayude y Santiago! Esta fue la primera vez y en aquel lugar que se hizo tal invocación en

---

3   Ibid., chapters V–VIII.

4   See R. A. Fletcher, "Saint James's Catapult: The Life and Times of Diego Gelmírez of Santiago de Compostela, Ciézar, Santiago Matamoros, Historia e Imagen," *Collección: Monografías,* No. 14, and Xosé Ramón Mariño Ferro's *Leyendas y Milagros del Camino de Santiago,*Graficas Varona, 2010.

España." ("May God help us and Saint James! This was the first time and in that place that such an invocation was made in Spain.").[5] Later it would become ¡Santiago y cierra España! (*Saint James and strike for Spain!*). The document may have been a forgery but the tribute that Ramiro vowed to make each year to Santiago continued until the early 1800s when it was abolished. The dictator Francisco Franco started it up again and you may be amused or surprised to know how Franco made the offering one year. But first a few facts are necessary to appreciate fully the story.

The fact is that Franco had a personal Moorish Guard until he died. That he had one as his body guard is not that unusual. Other leaders, such as the Cid, had Muslim support in battle. Enrique IV in the fifteenth century also had a Moorish Guard. Franco recruited about thirty thousand Muslims to aid him in the Spanish Civil War because of their fierceness in battle and their excellent horsemanship. After the war, he retained a regiment of these soldiers as his personal guard, known as the *Guardia Mora* (*Moorish Guard*) who served him until his death in 1975. Franco's guard was disbanded after his death since most of the original Muslim soldiers also had died. The regiment is still represented in military celebrations and parades today, but the soldiers are mainly Spanish who don the traditional dress of the Moorish Guard.

With the above facts in mind, the story goes like this. Franco reinstated the national *ofrenda* (*offering*) to Saint

5   Pedro Marcio, "El voto de Santiago" (www.ayuntamientodeclavijo. org/El-Voto-de-Santiago), English translation, mine.

James that was supposedly started by Ramiro I, as stated in the forged document of Marcio. Actually, several provincial kings during the middle ages contributed to Santiago de Compostela but King Phillip IV officially instituted it as a national offering in 1643 and it is still carried out by the present-day monarchs. It is a monetary tribute that is given by the State to the Cathedral of Santiago de Compostela and the ruler usually presides at the ceremony. However, one year Franco could not make it to Santiago for the annual tribute so he sent his Moroccan general, Mohamed ben Miziam del Qasim, to make the offering. Some thoughtful officials covered the base of Saint James's statue with cloth in order to hide the decapitated heads of the Moorish enemy. General Miziam del Qasim carried out his duty without any embarrassment to him or those around him.

My comments to this story are that this Muslim must have been very loyal to Franco or ignorant of the situation. I am presuming the former is true. This story may seem a bit bizarre, but in 2004, things became even stranger at the Cathedral of Santiago. The "politically correct" people decided that Saint James's statue of him as the "Moor Slayer" with Moorish severed heads at his feet was offensive to Moslems and ordered it removed from the Cathedral. This produced such an uproar among the fans of Saint James that the decision to remove the statue was overturned. Besides, if they removed this image how were they going to remove this same image that appears in thousands of locations throughout Spain? Some locations would have to be totally destroyed because many are sculpted over church portals. So a compromise was reached. Instead of removing the statue, they covered the Moors in flowers and Saint James appears to be riding though a garden of lilies. Outrageous! I do not believe history should be changed for the benefit of present-day politics, nor should later generations cover up those parts that may upset the changing sensibilities of the day. You cannot change the past and you should not even try. This is tantamount to denying the existence of the Jewish Holocaust of World War II. This statue should be shown without flowers and without politically correct guilt related to the victory over the Moors. The Moors were an invading army and brutal in their conquest of Spain. They occupied Spain for seven hundred years before eventually being thrown out. Shall we deny this too?

Stories and legends about Saint James the Moor Slayer flourished after the spread of the telling of the Battle of Clavijo. Various sources such as the *Codex* and chroniclers of the rulers relate these stories. One such story is Miracle 19 in the *Codex*, where Stephen, a Greek bishop, leaves his episcopal duties to visit the tomb of Saint James. He goes dressed as a pilgrim and not as a bishop. Upon arrival at the cathedral, he entreats the guards to give him an inconspicuous place in the church where he can offer continuous prayer. The guards agree and construct a cell-like structure for him in which he is able to look at the altar and keep vigil while praying.

One day a group of peasants enter and are standing near Stephan's hut. He hears one of the peasants refer to Saint James as a soldier and becomes outraged. He calls them stupid and foolish for calling James a soldier. To Stephan, James was a fisherman, and after called by the Lord, a "fisher of men."

The next night Saint James appears to Stephan dressed in white clothing bearing arms and holding two keys in his hand.

James tells Stephan that he is appearing to him in this fashion so that he will know that he is a fighter for God and is his champion. He further states that he does battle with Moors and leads Christians into battle against them. Then in order to convince Stephan he says that he will conquer the city of Coimbra currently held by the Moors and open the city's gates with the keys in his hand. He further states that it will happen the following day and tells him also the hour of victory.

On the following day Stephan calls the clerics and lay people together and he tells him what has transpired between Saint James and him. The day and hour that Stephan told to them matched those later sent by messengers from the king. Stephan then realizes that Saint James is more powerful and should be called upon to fight for the truth. Stephan decides to increase his praying and spends the rest of his life in this church. When he dies, he is buried in the church of his beloved Saint James.

The image of Saint James as warrior and Moor Slayer is further enhanced by the institution of Military Orders of the twelfth century. Included is the Order of Santiago founded in 1170. In Spain these Orders were instrumental in fighting the Moors during the Reconquest. Moreover, papal backing instructed Spanish rulers to treat the Reconquest like a crusade. In 1171, the Order of Santiago established an agreement with the Archbishop of Santiago that made them representatives and beneficiaries of Saint James. In 1180, the Order had spread throughout Castile, France, England, Portugal and Carinthia and was officially recognized by the pope. In ten years, Saint James and the Reconquest had become almost synonymous. You could not mention the one without the other.

This chapter started out with comments on the dichotomy of Saint James's character. One can see unity of his pilgrim nature with that of his warrior in yet another tale from the *Codex,* Book IV. Here, Saint James appears to Charlemagne in a dream telling him to do two things. First, establish the pilgrimage route to Santiago, and, secondly, take back the land lost to the Muslims. Thus, it is that the two characteristics of the saint achieve the same objective. As one scholar puts it, these two characteristics suggest "that contemporary Iberians could have seen pilgrimage and crusade as complementary elements of the same ideal."[6] In other words, there was no conflict between the two traits and they made his character complete or whole.

---

6   Rebecca C. Quinn, *Santiago as Matamoros: Race, Class, and Limpieza de Sangre in a Sixteenth-Century Spanish Manuscript*, (Southern Methodist University Digital Repository, http://digitalrepository.smu.edu/weil_ura/1, 2011), p. 21.

Epilogue

This book started as a journey across Northern Spain. Along the way stories of pain, humor, glory and gore were gathered. Some of these stories were ancient and others from the not too distant past. That these stories are still read or repeated today denotes their influence on the pilgrim, the Camino and Spain herself. I mentioned in the start of this book that the word *camino* would come to mean something different for every pilgrim. For me it is a long road of literary, historical, and legendary tales that I tried to relay to you. Yet I know that I have barely touched them. What I have given you is, as they say, "the tip of the iceberg." So many more tales are waiting to be heard, read or written down. Having been lured to the Camino by its rich cultural history and literature, I plan to be back on the Camino in the years to come searching for more stories and adventures. Since writing this book and about to send it to press, I have walked the Camino again to be sure I got my facts right and didn't imagine some of these far-out tales. Indeed, I may have uncovered more outlandish tales, but that is for another day or maybe another book.

Next year (2015) I hope to be back on the Camino somewhere as a volunteer *hospitalera (a person who aids pilgrims with information or works at a pilgrim lodging).* If anyone is interested in doing that, your first have to qualify by walking the Camino at least once. Knowing a foreign language also helps but is not required. It's also required that you take a three day class on the duties of a hospitalero. Currently you must commit to an assignment of two and a half weeks If interested, check out the American Piligrimage Association on line for more information.

One question I get asked is about miracles. Have I witnessed any or heard of any happening lately? Well, here's my very own miracle. I lost twenty-eight pounds, lowered my cholesterol by fifty-six points and my distance vision returned to 20/20. (I still have to use glasses or contact lenses for reading, but even that improved from a 4.25 power to 2.25 in contact lenses). My optometrist said it was due to all the walking and change in diet. I ate a lot of fresh vegetables and fish. One meal daily consisted of a huge salad loaded with fish, hard-boiled eggs and veggies. I never used dressing on the salad. All I can say is I never would have achieved these things at home. Thank you, Saint James!

Another question I am asked frequently is about lodging. How do I know where I will be spending the night? I would plan the day's walk one day ahead and then search for lodgings in the area where I would finish the walk. I used my iPad to find the lodgings and then after selecting one, I would either email the lodging for a reservation or have the concierge at my current lodging phone and make the reservation. Having the concierge make the arrangements was the fastest and most efficient way to do it. The concierge can arrange to have your backpack picked up and delivered to your next lodging if you want to be more comfortable on your walk. Currently it costs about seven euros or under ten dollars for this transportation. It is even less expensive as you get closer to Santiago, three euros. I did it a few times and never had a problem.

Here's something to ponder. As the pilgrimage continues to grow each year, so will new stories. What stories will be gleaned from these pilgrims in the next millennium?

If your curiosity has been roused enough with a few of these tales to seek out more and/or you have received some insight and/or entertainment from them, then I have done my job. Big thanks to you, dear reader, and *Buen Camino! Ultreya!*

Bibliography

Anon. *Nine Centuries of Spanish Literature*. New York: Dover Publications, Inc. Ed. by Seymour Resnick and Jeanne Pasmantier, 1994.

Anon. *Poem of My Cid* (Selections). Mineola, New York: Dover Publications, Edited and Translated by Stanley Appelbaum, 2005.

Bartha, Jeannie K., Annette Grant Cash, and Richard Terry Mount. *The Collected Works of Gonzalo de Berceo in English Translation*. Tempe: Arizona Center for Medieval and Renaissance Studies, 2008.

Berceo, Gonzalo de. *Miracles of Our Lady*, Translated by Richard Terry Mount and Annette Grant Cash. Lexington, KY: University of Kentucky Press, 1998.

Brault, Gerard J. *La Chanson de Roland*. University Park, PA: Pennsylvania State University, 1997.

Castro, Rosalía de. *The Poetry and Prose of Rosalía de Castro*. Lewiston, New York: The Edwin Mellen Press, trans. by Aileen Dever and John P. Dever, 2010.

Ciézar, Nicolás Cabrillana. "Santiago Matamoros, Historia e Imagen," *Collección: Monografías,* No. 14, Málaga:

Servicio de Publicaciones Diputación de Málaga, 1999.

Dunn, Maryjane. *"Nationalism, Regionalism and Faith in the Works of Emilia Pardo Bazán: St. James and the Pilgrimage to Santiago de Compostela, 1880–1920," Ad Limina*, Vol. 4, No. 4, 2013.

Coffey, Thomas F., Linda Kay Davidson, and Maryjane Dunn. *The Miracles of Saint James.* New York: Italica Press, 1996.

Díaz y Díaz, Manual C., María Araceli García Piñeiro, and Pilar del Oro Trigo. *El Códice Calixtino de la Catedral de Santiago: Estudio codicológico y de contenido.* Santiago de Compostela: Centro de Estudios Jacobeos, 1988.

Fletcher, R. A. "Saint James's Catapult: The Life and Times of Diego Gelmírez of Santiago de Compostela, Ciézar, Santiago Matamoros, Historia e Imagen," *Collección: Monografías,* No. 14, Málaga: Servicio de Publicaciones Diputación de Málaga, 1999.

Ferro, Xosé Ramón Mariño. *Leyendas y Milagros del Camino de Santiago.* Graficas Varona. 2010.

Gitlitz David M. and Linda Kay Davidson. *The Pilgrimage Road to Santiago.* New York: St. Martin's Griffin, 2000.

Hemingway, Ernest. *The Sun Also Rises.* New York: Scribner, 2006 ed.

Herlihy-Mera, Jeffrey. "'He Was Sort of a Joke, In Fact': Ernest Hemingway in Spain." *The Hemingway Review*, Vol. 31, No. 2, 2012.

Isidore, Saint. *Isidore of Seville's Etymologies: the complete English translation of Isidori Hispalensis Episcopi Etymologiarum sive Originum Libri xx Volume 1.* Charlotte, Vermont, trans. by Pricilla Throop, 2005.

Keister, Douglas. *Stories in Stone: A Field Guide to Cemetery Symbolism and Iconography.* Salt Lake City, UT: Gibbs Smith, 2004.

Kulp-Hill, Kathleen, *Songs of Holy Mary of Alfonso X, the Wise.* Tempe: Arizona Center for Medieval and Renaissance Studies, 2000.

Lacalla, María Jesús. *"Cuentos Y Leyendas en el Camino De Santiago."* Zaragosa: Intitución Fernando El Católico, 2005. (Article found on internet.)

LaPrada, Douglas Edward. *Hemingway & Franco.* Universitat de Valencia, 2007.

Marcio, Pedro. *"El voto de Santiago."* www.ayuntamientodeclavijo.org/El-Voto-de-Santiago

Melczer William, *The Pilgrim's Guide to Santiago de Compostela.* New York: Italica Press, 1993.

Moore, Jr., John K. *"Juxtaposing James the Greater: Interpreting the Interstices of Santiago as Peregrino and Matamoros."* University of Alabama at Birmingham:

Mervyn H. Sterne Library, Project Muse, 2010. (Article found on internet.)

Pardo Bazán, Emilia, "La danza del peregrino." *Boletín de la Asociación Gaditana del Camino de Santiago,* Núm. 8, enero, 2011.

Quesada-Embid Mercedes C. *"Dwelling, Walking, Serving: Organic Preservation Along the Camino de Santiago Pilgrimage Landscape."* Antioch University New England, 2008.

Quevedo y Villegas, Francisco de. *Obras de Don Francisco de Quevedo Villegas.* Madrid: M. Rivadeneyra, 1859.

———————————. *El Buscón.* Madrid: Lável Artes Gráficas, 2011.

———————————. *Two Spanish Picaresque Novels (Lazarillo de Tormes and The Swindler).* London: Penguin Books, translated by Michael Alpert. 1988.

Quinn, Rebecca C. *"Santiago as Matamoros: Race, Class, and Limpieza de Sangre in a Sixteenth-Century Spanish Manuscript."* Southern Methodist University Digital Repository. http://digitalrepository.smu.edu/weil_ ura/1, 2011

Robert Southey. "The Pilgrim to Santiago," www.pricejb.pwp. blueyonder.co.uk/ Transcribed by John Price, 2006.

Smyser, H W. *The Pseudo Turpin.* Cambridge: The Medieval Academy of America, 1937.

Index

Page numbers in **Bold** refer to photographs.

About the Author

Jean Mitchell Lanham is a pilgrim currently living near San Francisco. She received her PhD from The Ohio State University in 1977 in Romance languages and literature with a concentration in Spanish medieval literature. She pursued graduate studies in both Mexico and Madrid, has taught at several major universities, and traveled extensively worldwide. Her other interests are underwater photography, martial arts, and adopting unwanted Dalmatians. Her latest feat was to complete the 500-mile pilgrim's route to Santiago, where she did research for this book. If anyone would like to contact Jean, you may do so via her email: lanhammitchell@hotmail.com